Access 2007: Basic

Crisp Comprehensive Series

CRISP

Access 2007: Basic

President, Axzo Press:	Jon Winder
Vice President, Product Development:	Charles G. Blum
Vice President, Operations:	Josh Pincus
Director of Publishing Systems Development:	Dan Quackenbush
Writer:	Don Tremblay
Developmental Editor:	Steve English
Copyeditor:	Robert Tillett
Keytester:	Cliff Coryea

For more information, go to www.axzopress.com.

Trademarks

Disclaimer

ISBN 10: 1-4260-1920-3
ISBN 13: 978-1-4260-1920-3

Printed in the United States of America

1 2 3 4 5 6 7 8 9 10 GL 12 11 10

Contents

Introduction

After reading this introduction, you will know how to:

A Use Crisp Comprehensive learning solutions in general.

B Use prerequisites, a target student description, course objectives, and a skills inventory to properly set your expectations for the course.

C Set up your computer to run the course.

Topic A: About the Crisp Comprehensive series

Our philosophy

The Crisp Comprehensive series combines the training industry's leading course manuals, expert video instruction, online mentoring, and assessment software into a total, all-in-one learning solution.

We believe strongly in the instructor-led class, but there isn't always the time or the opportunity. The Crisp Comprehensive series is the next best thing—it puts you in control, with an interactive instructional video to accompany the course manual. As you work through the video, you'll have the opportunity to practice the skills covered in the book. Online mentoring gives you the ability to "raise your hand" for further assistance. And you can test your progress with the assessment software.

Learning solution components

Crisp Comprehensive learning solutions contain these major components:

- Course manual
- Instructional video on DVD
- Online mentoring
- Assessment software

Each element is described below.

Course manual

Our manuals are divided into units, with each unit containing several related topics. While we provide text to explain important concepts, the hands-on activities are the focus of our courses. Each unit concludes with review questions to test your learning.

Instructional video

Included on the DVD in the front of this book, the instructional video leads you through each and every concept and activity covered in the course. The intuitive user interface enables you to pause, rewind, and fast-forward the instruction to suit your needs. After launching the video, click the Introduction link for an overview on navigating the various components of the video.

Online mentoring

Online mentoring provides real-time guidance from knowledgeable instructors over a period of six months. See the sticker on the DVD envelope to learn how.

CertBlaster assessment software

The CertBlaster assessment software is geared toward students who are planning to take the Microsoft Certified Application Specialist exam for Access 2007. Therefore, it includes some questions that are beyond the scope of this course. It's still a great tool to test what you've learned and to see what you might want to learn next.

To download and install your free software:

1. Go to **www.axzopress.com/certblaster**.
2. Under Downloads, click Certblaster.
3. Click the link for Access 2007.
4. Save the .EXE file to a folder on your hard drive. (Note: If you skip this step, the CertBlaster software will not install correctly.)
5. Click Start and choose Run.
6. Click Browse and navigate to the folder that contains the .EXE file.
7. Select the .EXE file and click Open.
8. Click OK and follow the on-screen instructions. When prompted for the password, enter **c_605**.

Manual conventions

Here are some conventions and icons you should know about.

Item	Description
Italic text	In conceptual text, indicates a new term or feature.
Bold text	In unit summaries, indicates a key term or concept. In an independent practice activity, indicates an explicit item that you select, choose, or type.
`Code font`	Indicates code or syntax.

`Longer strings of ▶`
`code will look ▶`
`like this.`
	In the hands-on activities, any code that's too long to fit on a single line is divided into segments by one or more continuation characters (▶). This code should be entered as a continuous string of text.

Select **bold item**	In the left column of hands-on activities, bold sans-serif text indicates an explicit item that you select, choose, or type.
Keycaps like ↵ ENTER	Indicate a key on the keyboard you must press.

Hands-on activities

The hands-on activities are the most important parts of our manuals. They are divided into two primary columns. The "Here's how" column gives short instructions to you about what to do. The "Here's why" column provides explanations, graphics, and clarifications. Here's a sample:

Do it!

A-1: Creating a commission formula

Here's how	Here's why
1 Open Sales	This is an oversimplified sales compensation worksheet. It shows sales totals, commissions, and incentives for five sales reps.
2 Observe the contents of cell F4	 The commission rate formulas use the name "C_Rate" instead of a value for the commission rate.

For these activities, we have provided a collection of data files designed to help you learn each skill in a real-world business context. As you work through the activities, you will modify and update these files. If you make a mistake and want to re-key an activity, starting from scratch, you can. To make it easy to start over, you will rename each data file at the end of the first activity in which the file is modified. Our convention for renaming files is to add the word "My" to the beginning of the file name. In the above activity, for example, a file called "Sales" is being used for the first time. At the end of this activity, you would save the file as "My sales," thus leaving the "Sales" file unchanged. If you make a mistake, you can start over, using the original "Sales" file.

Topic B: Setting your expectations

Properly setting your expectations is essential to your success. This topic will help you do that by providing:

- Prerequisites for this course
- A description of the target student
- A list of the objectives for the course
- A skills assessment for the course

Course prerequisites

Before running this course, you should be familiar with personal computers and the use of a keyboard and a mouse. Furthermore, this course assumes that you are comfortable working with the Microsoft Windows operating system.

Target student

The target student for this course is interested in learning how to use the basic features of Access 2007 to create tables, forms, reports, and filters.

Microsoft Certified Application Specialist certification

This course is designed for the working professional who wants to learn the fundamentals of Access 2007. However, if you're interested in taking the Microsoft Certified Application Specialist exam for Access 2007, we've provided some additional information to help you study. Specifically, the certification objectives covered in this course are listed at the beginning of each topic (where applicable). The CertBlaster assessment software also includes more advanced questions typical of those found on the exam.

Course objectives

These overall objectives will give you an idea about what to expect from the course. It is also possible that they will help you see that this course is not the right one for you.

After completing this course, you will know how to:

- Organize data efficiently by using a database management system; start Access and open Access databases; and use the Help feature.
- Plan and create a database; use Datasheet view and Design view; and create tables and work in tables.
- Modify a table's design; use the attachment data type; find and replace data; sort, filter, and delete records.
- Set field properties, create input masks, and set validation rules.
- Create queries, and sort and filter the results; modify queries; and perform operations in queries.
- Create, modify, and work with forms; and use them to sort and filter records.
- Create reports by using the Report button, the Report Wizard, Design view, Layout view, and queries; modify and print reports.

Skills inventory

Use the following form to gauge your skill level before running the course. For each skill listed, rate your familiarity from 1 to 5, with 5 being the most familiar. *This is not a test*. Rather, it is intended to provide you with an idea of where you're starting from so you can focus on the skills you most need to learn.

Skill	1	2	3	4	5
Identifying database components					
Starting and examining Access					
Opening a database					
Examining the Database window and a database table					
Using Help					
Planning and creating a database					
Examining a table in Datasheet view and Design view					
Creating a table by using the Table Wizard and Design view					
Adding fields to a table, and setting the primary key					
Creating a composite key					
Saving and adding records					
Modifying field names, and deleting and inserting fields					
Finding and replacing values in a table					
Sorting records					
Filtering records					
Setting field properties					
Creating an input mask					
Creating queries by using the Query Wizard and Design view					
Sorting and filtering query results					
Using comparison operators and calculations in a query					
Creating and modifying forms					
Sorting and filtering records in a form					
Creating reports					
Grouping and summarizing data in a report					
Printing a report					

Topic C: Technical requirements

This topic lists the hardware and software requirements for your personal computer. It also provides information on how to set up your computer to run the course.

The Windows operating system and the Office 2007 suite are subject to continual updating by Microsoft, so the setup process described here might vary slightly from what you will encounter. Activities and screen shots throughout the course might vary slightly as well.

Hardware requirements

Your personal computer should have:

- A keyboard and a mouse
- A Pentium 500 MHz processor (or higher)
- 256 MB RAM (or higher)
- 4 GB of available hard drive space
- A DVD drive
- An SVGA monitor set to 1024×768 resolution, or higher
- A printer is required to complete Activity C-3 in Unit 8

Software requirements

You will also need the following software:

- Windows XP, Windows Vista, Windows 7, or Windows Server 2003
- Microsoft Office 2007

Network requirements

Internet access is needed to:

- Update the Windows operating system and Office 2007 at update.microsoft.com
- Open Help files at Microsoft Office Online. (If online Help is not available, you will not be able to complete Activity C-1 in Unit 1.)
- Download document templates from Microsoft Office Online. (If online templates are not available, students will not be able to complete activity C-1 in Unit 2.).

Course setup instructions

Before you begin the course, you will need to perform the following steps.

1 Install Windows XP on an NTFS partition according to the software manufacturer's instructions.

   Note: You can also use Windows Vista or Windows Server 2003, but the screen shots in this course were taken using Windows XP, so your screens will look somewhat different.

2 If the operating system is Windows XP, then launch the Control Panel, open the Display Properties dialog box and apply the following settings:
   - Theme—Windows XP
   - Screen resolution—1024 by 768 pixels
   - Color quality—High (24 bit) or higher

3 If Windows was already loaded on this PC, verify that Internet Explorer is the default Web browser. (If you installed Windows yourself, skip this step.)
   a Click Start, All Programs, Internet Explorer.
   b Choose Tools, Internet Options.
   c Check "Internet Explorer should check to see whether it is the default browser."
   d Click OK to close the Internet Options dialog box.
   e Close and re-open Internet Explorer.
   f If a prompt appears, asking you to make Internet Explorer your default browser, click Yes.
   g Close Internet Explorer.

4 Open Internet Explorer and navigate to **update.microsoft.com**. Update the operating system with the latest critical updates and service packs.

5 Install Microsoft Office 2007 according to the software manufacturer's instructions, as follows:
   a When prompted for the CD key, enter the code included with your software.
   b Select the Customize installation option and click Next.
   c Activate the Installation Options tab.
   d For Access 2007, Office Shared Features, and Office Tools, click the drop-down arrow and choose Run all from My Computer.
   e Set all but the following to Not Available: Access 2007, Office Shared Features, and Office Tools.
   f Click Install Now.
   g On the last screen of the Office 2007 installer, click Go to Office Online. Internet Explorer displays the Office Online Web site, and the installer window closes.
   h On the Office Online Web page, activate the Downloads tab.
   i Download and install any available updates.
   j Close Internet Explorer.

6 Create a folder named Student Data at the root of the hard drive. For a standard hard drive setup, this will be C:\Student Data.

7 Copy the files from the data CD in the back of this book to C:\Student Data.

8 Start Access 2007.

  a Activate the software. After activating, the Welcome to the 2007 Microsoft Office System dialog box appears.

  b On the Privacy Options screen, verify that "Search Microsoft Office Online for Help content when I'm connected to the Internet" is checked.

  c Verify that "Download a file periodically that helps determine system problems" is cleared.

  d Verify that "Sign up for the Customer Experience Improvement Program" is cleared.

  e Click Next.

  f Select "I don't want to use Microsoft Update."

  g Click Finish to close the dialog box.

9 To ensure that you won't get a security warning when you open files in Access 2007, designate the student data folder as a Trusted Location:

  a Click the Office Button and choose Access Options to open the Access Options dialog box.

  b On the Trust Center page, click Trust Center Settings. The Trust Center dialog box opens.

  c Navigate to the Trusted Locations page.

  d Click Add new location. The Microsoft Office 2007 Trusted Location dialog box opens.

  e Click Browse and navigate to the student data folder.

  f Click OK to close the Browse dialog box.

  g Check Subfolders of this location are also trusted.

  h Click OK to close the Microsoft Office 2007 Trusted Location dialog box.

  i Click OK to close the Trust Center dialog box.

10 Make the student data folder the default file location.

  a In the left panel of the Access Options dialog box, choose Popular.

  b Under Creating databases, click Browse, and navigate to the student data folder.

  c Click OK to close the Default Database Path dialog box.

  d Click OK to close the Access Options dialog box.

  e Close Access 2007.

Unit 1
Getting started

Complete this unit, and you'll know how to:

A Organize data efficiently by using a database management system.

B Start Access, learn about its environment, open a database file with shared access, and learn about database objects.

C Use Help options to get information on Access topics.

Topic A: Database concepts

Explanation

Microsoft Access 2007, a component of the Microsoft Office suite, is a database management program, an application that stores and organizes data and makes data retrieval efficient. A *database* is a collection of data, or information. An example of a simple database is a phone book that contains the names, phone numbers, and addresses of individuals and businesses.

Database components

The following table defines several database-related terms used in Access:

Term	Description
Data value	An item of data. In Exhibit 1-1, 2 oz is a data value.
Record	All of the data values that apply to a specific item listed in the table. In Exhibit 1-1, each row in the table is a record that contains all data for a single spice.
Field	A specific type of data that applies to each item listed in the table. In Exhibit 1-1, each column in the table is a field that contains data values for each spice. For example, Field 3 contains the price of each spice.
Table	A collection of records. The records and fields in a table form its rows and columns. Exhibit 1-1 shows a simple table named tblProduct. It contains four fields and ten records.

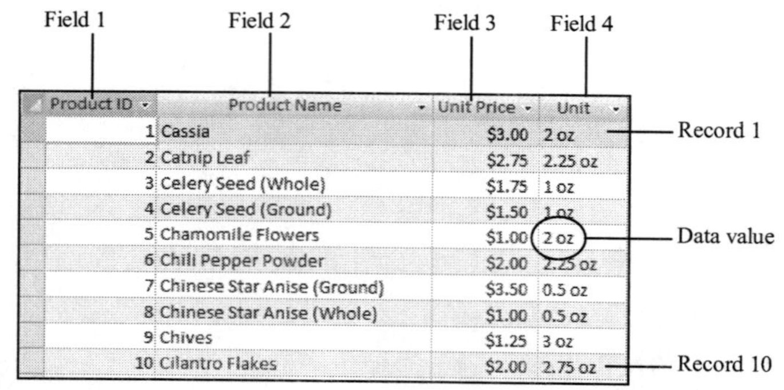

Product ID	Product Name	Unit Price	Unit
1	Cassia	$3.00	2 oz
2	Catnip Leaf	$2.75	2.25 oz
3	Celery Seed (Whole)	$1.75	1 oz
4	Celery Seed (Ground)	$1.50	1 oz
5	Chamomile Flowers	$1.00	2 oz
6	Chili Pepper Powder	$2.00	2.25 oz
7	Chinese Star Anise (Ground)	$3.50	0.5 oz
8	Chinese Star Anise (Whole)	$1.00	0.5 oz
9	Chives	$1.25	3 oz
10	Cilantro Flakes	$2.00	2.75 oz

Exhibit 1-1: The tblProduct table

Do it!

A-1: Identifying database components

Here's how	Here's why
1 Observe the table	As shown in Exhibit 1-1. This table contains ten rows and four columns.
2 Observe the column headings	The headings are Product ID, Product Name, Unit Price, and Unit. Each column represents a field.
3 Observe the data values in each field	Each field contains a specific type of data value.
4 Observe the rows	Each row contains data for a single product. For example, the fifth row contains the record for chamomile flowers.

Relational databases

Explanation

Microsoft Access creates a *relational database*, in which data is organized in related tables. In related tables, one or more fields are linked to fields in another table. This link ensures that you can enter only those values that have corresponding entries in the other table. For example, suppose that you store product details and sales details in two tables. These tables can be related by using the common field ProductID. This ensures that you cannot enter the sales details of any products that are not available in the product details table.

A relational database can have multiple tables that contain data about various entities, such as products, sales, or customers. An *entity* is any object that has a distinct set of properties. A relational database helps you store data in an orderly manner so that you can retrieve it efficiently. For example, if you need to display the product details and sales details in a single report, you can access the corresponding tables to get the information.

Do it!

A-2: Identifying the advantages of relational databases

Questions and answers

1 What is a relational database?

2 Microsoft Access creates relational databases. True or false?

3 What are the advantages of using a relational database?

Topic B: Exploring the Access environment

This topic covers the following Microsoft Certified Application Specialist exam objective for Access 2007.

#	Objective
6.1.1	**Open databases** • With shared access

Components of the Access window

Explanation

You start Access by choosing Start, All Programs, Microsoft Office, Microsoft Office Access 2007. The Getting Started screen, shown in Exhibit 1-2, offers a number of database templates that can be used to start databases. Some templates are included with the application while others have to be downloaded from the Internet. There are also options to start a new blank database or open recently used databases.

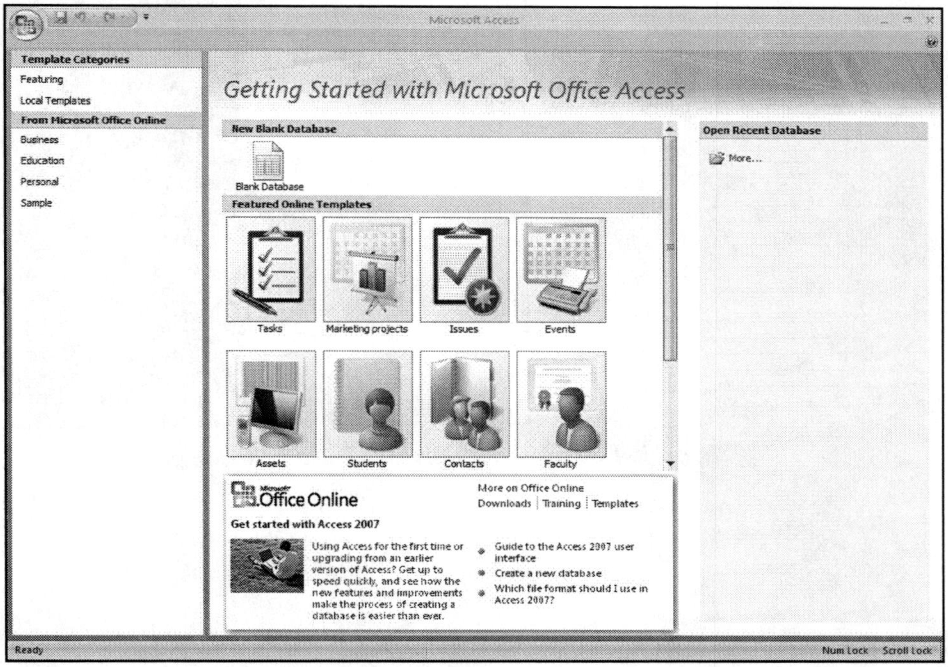

Exhibit 1-2: The Access 2007 Getting Started screen

Most of your time, however, won't be spent looking at the opening screen; it will be spent working on databases via the user interface.

The Ribbon user interface

Access 2007 uses a Ribbon interface to display commands and options. The Ribbon is divided into tabs. When you activate a tab, commands and icons appear on the Ribbon. These are context sensitive—they change depending on what object (a form, a table, a report, etc.) is opened and in what view.

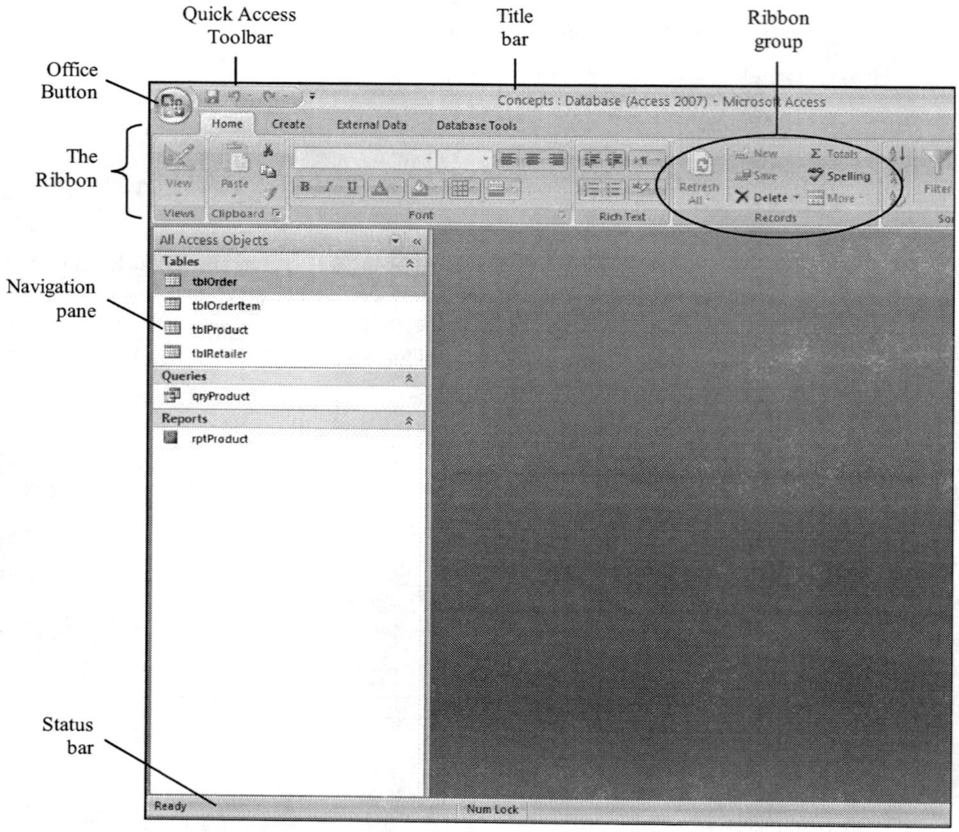

Exhibit 1-3: An open database and the Ribbon interface

The following table describes the components of the Access window:

Item	Description
Office Button	Contains commands for opening, saving, managing, sending, and printing a database; and exiting the program. Also contains the Access Options button, which opens the Access Options dialog box.
Quick Access Toolbar	Contains frequently used commands such as Save, Print, and Undo. Can be customized to include the commands you wish.
Title bar	Displays the name of the current database.
Ribbon group	Contains menus, commands, lists, and galleries.
The Ribbon	Contains tabs that are divided into groups.
Navigation pane	Lists tables, queries, forms, reports, and other database objects. The type of object is selected from the drop-down list at the top of the pane. Click the double arrow in the pane's upper right corner to expand and collapse it.
Status bar	When a table, query, report, or other database object is open, it contains the status messages, View buttons, and the document zoom slider.

Do it!

B-1: Starting Access and examining the Access window

Here's how	Here's why
1 Choose **Start**, **All Programs**, **Microsoft Office**, **Microsoft Office Access 2007**	(To start Access.) The Microsoft Access window appears, as shown in Exhibit 1-2.
Maximize the window	If necessary.
2 Observe the Getting Started screen	There's the Office Button, a pane of template categories, icons for templates, an icon to create a blank database, a list of recently opened databases, and links to resources from Office Online.
3 Click 	(The Office Button is in the top left corner of the application window.) The File menu opens.
Observe the commands and options on the File menu	
4 Click **Access Options**	To open the Access Options dialog box.
Select various categories in the left pane and observe the settings that are available for change.	Don't make any changes at this time.
5 Click **Cancel**	To close the dialog box.

Opening databases

Explanation

To open an existing database, you use the Open dialog box. This dialog box can be opened in any of these ways:

- Click the Office Button, and choose Open.
- Press Ctrl-O.
- On the Open Recent Database pane, click the database name or click More to browse for the database.

In the Open dialog box, specify the name of the folder and database you want to open, and then click the Open button. You can also double-click the file name.

File formats

When you open or create a database, its file format appears on the title bar in square brackets after the database name. The *file format* is the specific format in which each application stores data. By default, Access 2007 creates databases in the Access 2007 file format with the extension .accdb. A database created in Access 2007 format cannot be opened in earlier versions of Access, but Access 2007 can work with earlier formats. For backward compatibility, files can be saved in Access 2002-2003 format or in Access 2000 format.

Shared access

When you open a database file, it opens by default with shared access. This means that while you are editing and changing the database, other users can open and edit it at the same time.

Do it!

B-2: Opening a database

Here's how	Here's why
1 Click 	The Office Button.
Choose **Open**	The Open dialog box appears.
2 Navigate to the current unit folder within the Student Data folder	To display the files in the current unit folder.
Select **Concepts**	(If necessary.) You'll open this database.
Click **Open**	
3 Observe the Access title bar	The title bar displays "Concepts : Database (Access 2007)."
4 Observe the Ribbon	It has different tabs for categories of commands. Related commands on each tab are placed together in Groups.

Navigating a database

Explanation

When a database opens, the name and format of the database appears in the title bar, and the Navigation Pane opens on the left side of the Access window, as shown in Exhibit 1-3.

The Navigation Pane displays the objects in your database. Objects include tables, forms, queries, and reports. You can use the Navigation Pane to change which objects display and in what order. For instance, you can display just tables, or all objects.

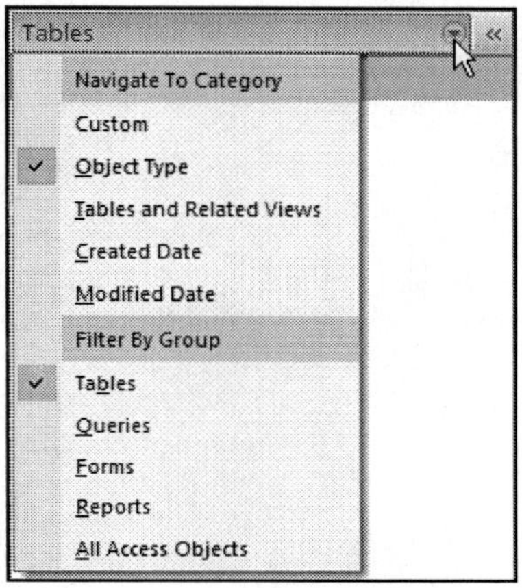

Exhibit 1-4: The Navigation Pane showing options

Access database objects

The following table describes the objects in an Access database:

Object	Description
Table	Stores data. For example, you can use a table to store details about employees, such as name, title, and department.
Query	Retrieves specific information—such as which product had the highest sales for a given month, or which employees work in the Western region—from a table.
Form	Enters data into a table in a database. You can use a form to view and modify records in a table.
Report	Prints or displays data. You can customize a report by applying different font styles and headings.
Macro	Automates frequently performed database tasks, such as printing a set of weekly reports.
Module	Automates and customizes database operations. Modules are programs written in Visual Basic.

Do it!

B-3: Using the Navigation Pane

Here's how	Here's why
1 Observe the Navigation Pane	On the left side of the window. It shows the tables in the database. Tables, reports, forms, and other items in Access are called objects.
2 On the Navigation Pane, click **Tables**	You'll see the drop-down menu shown in Exhibit 1-4. Here you can select which objects you'll see in the pane.
Choose **All Access Objects**	All the objects appear in the Navigation Pane, and the top of the pane now reads All Access Objects. In addition to the tables, you also see a query and a report.
3 Click **All Access Objects** and choose **Modified Date**	All the objects appear in the order of modification, with the latest at the top.
4 Click **All Dates**	The drop down menu now reads All Dates to indicate that the objects are ordered by date.
Observe the menu	It now shows options to specify which objects to show based on how old they are.
5 Show only tables in the Navigation Pane	Use the menu to select object types and then tables.
6 Click the double arrow in the upper right of the Navigation Pane, as shown	 To collapse the pane and give you more room to work.
Expand the pane	Click the double arrow.

Open a database table

Explanation

You open a table to view and edit its contents. To open any database object, double-click the object's name in the Navigation Pane. Double-clicking will open a table in Datasheet view, as opposed to Design view or any other view that might be available.

If you open multiple tables or other objects, Access 2007 displays them as a series of tabbed documents. You can change this default to hide all but the active object.

Do it!

B-4: Examining a database table

Here's how	Here's why
1 In the Navigation Pane, double-click **tblProduct**	You'll view the contents of this table.
2 Observe the headings in the Table window	The table has four fields. The field headings are Product ID, Product Name, Unit Price, and Unit.
3 Observe the rows and columns in the table	Each row corresponds to a record, and each column corresponds to a field.
4 Click the close window button.	(The X button in the upper right corner of the table) To close the table.
5 Click the Office Button and choose **Close Database**	To close the database. The Getting Started screen appears.

Topic C: Getting help

Explanation

The Help button is on the right side of the Ribbon. When you choose Help, Access Help tries first to connect via the Internet to Help files at Microsoft Office Online, as shown in Exhibit 1-5. This ensures that you are using the most current Help files. While connected to Office Online, Help can also download templates or display training files. If Help cannot connect to Office Online, it loads Help files installed on your computer, as shown in Exhibit 1-6.

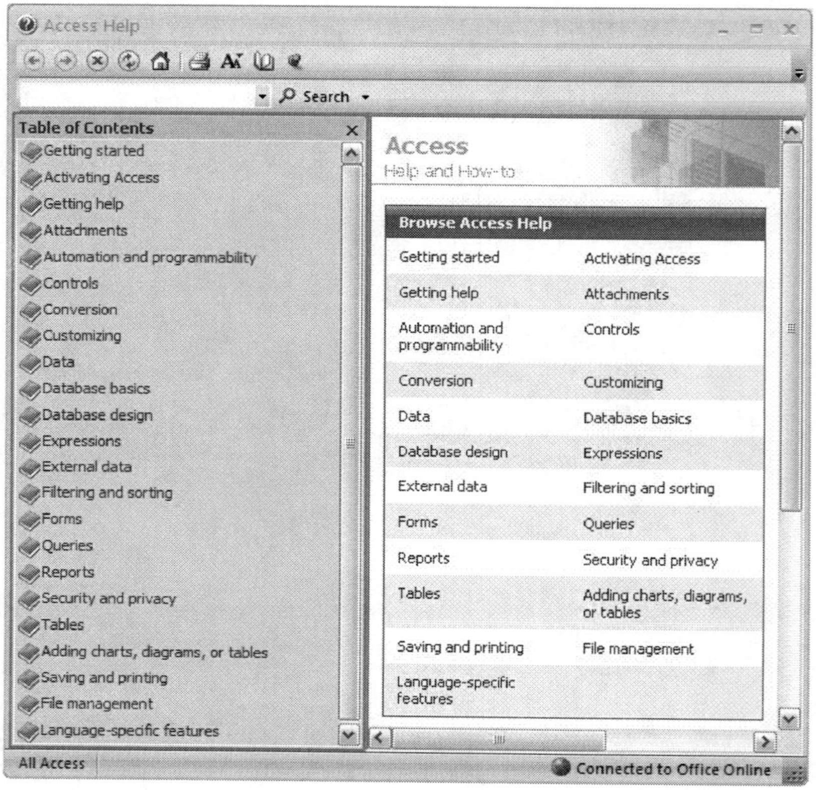

Exhibit 1-5: Access Help, connected to Help files at Office Online

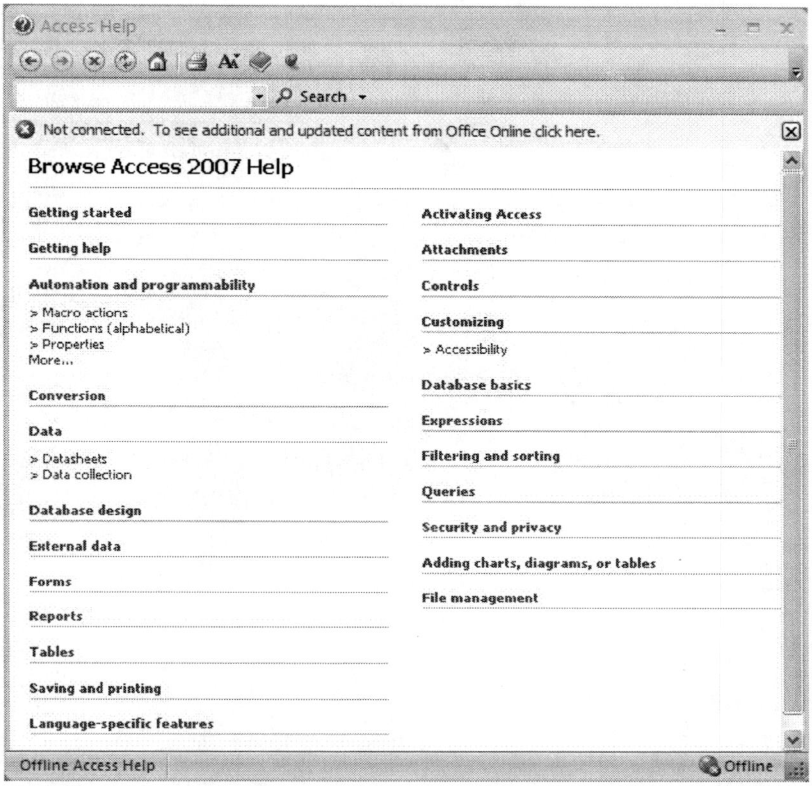

Exhibit 1-6: Access Help, using offline content stored on the computer

To search for Help, type a question or keyword in the box and click Search. A list of corresponding help topics appears in the right pane of the Help window. Select a topic from the list to view detailed information.

If Help is connected to Office Online, you can also select a Help topic from the Table of Contents in the right pane. Detailed information appears in the right pane.

Do it!

C-1: Using Help

Here's how	Here's why
1 Click 	(The Microsoft Office Access Help button is on the right side of the Ribbon.) You'll search for information related to the term "database."
In the Search box, enter **database**	(The Search box is near the upper left corner of the window.) To enter a search term.
Click Search	To search the Help files at Microsoft Office Online. A list of related topics appears.
2 Click **Database design basics**	The window displays Help on the selected topic.
3 Close the Microsoft Access Help window	In the Access Help window, click the close button.

Unit summary: Getting started

Topic A

In this topic, you learned that a **database** stores data in the form of **tables**. You learned that a table contains **records** and **fields**. You also learned about **relational databases**, which store data in related tables.

Topic B

In this topic, you learned how to start Access and you examined the **Microsoft Access** window. You learned about the **Navigation Pane**, which is used to specify which database objects you see, and in what order. You also learned how to open a database file with **shared access**.

Topic C

In this topic, you learned how to use the **Help** feature to access online Help or offline Help files.

Review questions

1 Identify the correct term for each of the following:

Description	Term
A set of related data values	
A collection of records	
An item of data	

2 Let's say you're working with a database that contains information about the salespeople at Outlander Spices. Which object you would use for each of the following tasks?

Task	Database object
Enter information for a new salesperson.	
Find departments with earnings of more than $80,000.	
Print all values from the table.	

3 What is a relational database?

4 Name two sources used by the Help system.

5 What is shared access?

Independent practice activity

In this activity, you'll identify Access components, open a database and identify database objects, then open a table. Next, you'll close the table and close the database.

1 Open PracticeConcepts (from the current unit folder).

2 In the Access window, identify the Navigation Pane.

3 Identify the types and number of database objects in the database. (*Hint*: Choose All Access Objects from the Navigation Pane menu.)

4 Open the tblEmployee table. How many fields and records are there in this table?

5 Close the tblEmployee table.

6 Close the PracticeConcepts database.

Unit 2

Databases and tables

Complete this unit, and you'll know how to:

A Plan and create a database.

B Examine a table in Datasheet view and Design view.

C Create and modify tables; create a primary key and a composite key.

Topic A: Planning and designing databases

This topic covers the following Microsoft Certified Application Specialist exam objectives for Access 2007.

#	Objective
1.1.1	**Define table fields** • Establish which data needs to be stored and which should be calculated at run time
2.1.1	**Create databases by using templates**
2.1.2	**Create blank databases**

Planning databases

Explanation

Before creating a database, it's important to plan the type of data to be stored. For example, if you're keeping track of a company's products, sales, and retailers, you must plan and design a database that can store the related data. This data should be stored in three separate tables so you can distinguish between these three sets of information. You'll also need to plan how you'll be using the information stored in the database. Thorough planning ensures that no data is missing or redundant, and it saves time on future modifications to the database.

To plan a database, you must determine:

- The purpose of the database
- The number of tables and the type of information you'll store in each table
- The fields that will be used in each table
- The types of queries you'll want to perform on the database
- The forms you'll need to create
- The types of reports you'll need to generate

Stored vs. calculated

When planning a database, you should determine which data should be *stored*, and which data should be *calculated* at run time. Stored data remains the same until a user changes it. Calculated data changes in response to other database updates.

For example, the price of an individual spice is typically a stored value; that is, it remains the same until a user changes it. But the total value of a spice held in inventory changes when the price does: if the price goes up, the value in inventory increases, and vice versa. The total inventory value, which depends on the price, is an example of data that should be calculated by the database rather than entered by the user.

Do it!

A-1: Planning a database

Questions and answers

1 You work in the Sales and Marketing department of Outlander Spices. You keep track of the company's retailers, and you want to create a database of information related to the operations in your department. What is the purpose of the database?

2 While creating the database, how many tables will you need to create, and what type of information do you need to store in each table?

3 Identify some of the fields that you'll need to create in the tables.

4 What kind of information could you extract from these tables by using queries?

5 If a database field tracks the quantity sold to a retailer, should that data be stored or calculated at run time?

6 If a database field tracks the number of days outstanding for a retailer's invoice, should that data be stored or calculated at run time?

Creating a database

Explanation

After you've planned and designed a database, you're ready to create it. A database can be created from a template or by starting with a blank database.

Rules for naming databases and objects

When naming a database or any database object, observe the following naming conventions:

- The name can contain letters, numbers, special characters, and embedded spaces.
- The name cannot contain more than 64 characters.
- The name cannot start with a space.

It's good practice to use an underscore (_) instead of an embedded space in a database name or an object name. Object names cannot include a period (.), an exclamation mark (!), an accent grave (`), or brackets ([]).

Database templates

Access has database templates designed for various tasks. Some of these come with Access while others can be downloaded. If you find a template that seems to fit your purpose, it can be used to create a new database and then adjusted to suit your needs.

To create a database by using a template:

1. On the Getting Started screen, observe the template categories listed on the left.
2. Select a template category.
3. Select the template that most closely describes what you need.
4. In the right pane, name the database.
5. Click Create, or, if the template is online, click Download.

Do it!

A-2: Creating a database from a template

Here's how	Here's why
1 On the Getting Started screen, under Featured Online Templates, click **Contacts**	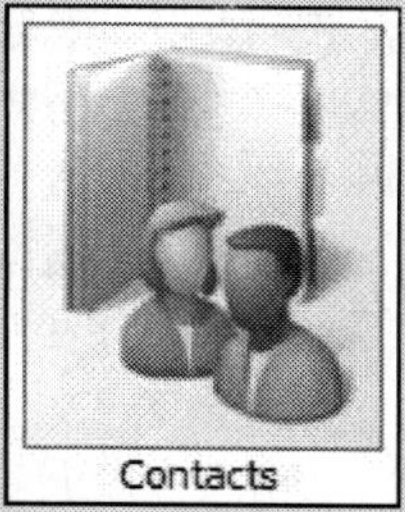 Template names and icons appear in the middle of the window.
2 In the right pane, click the browse icon, as shown	 The File New Database dialog box appears. You'll specify a location for the file.
Browse to the current unit folder	
3 Edit the file name to read **MyContacts**	
Click **OK**	To close the dialog box. The location shown under the file name is now the current unit folder.
4 Click **Download**	To save and open the new database. The database opens and displays the Contact List.
5 Click **OK**	(If necessary.) To accept the genuine Windows agreement.
Close the Help window	If necessary.
Observe the Contact List menu bar	(It's above the field names.) It has options for creating new contacts or adding them from Outlook.
6 Close the database	Click the Office Button and choose Close Database. MyContacts now appears in the Open Recent Database list.

Creating blank databases

Explanation

When you create a blank database, you'll initially see only the Database window. You must then manually create the objects to include in the database. This manual method is more flexible because it results in custom tables and fields, instead of using a predefined design provided by a template.

To create a blank Access database:

1. Click the Office Button. The Getting Started window displays Blank Database in the right pane.
2. Specify the location and the name of the database.
3. Click Create.

Do it!

A-3: Creating a blank database

Here's how	Here's why
1 Click 	(The Office Button is in the upper-left corner of the Access 2007 window.) To display the file commands.
Choose **New**	The Getting Started window displays, with Blank Database in the right pane.
2 In the right pane, edit the file name to read **CreateDatabase**	
Navigate to the current unit folder	
3 Click **Create**	The database opens to an empty table in Datasheet view. The title bar reads CreateDatabase : Database (Access 2007).
4 Click 	
Choose **Close Database**	To close the database.

Topic B: Exploring tables

This topic covers the following Microsoft Certified Application Specialist exam objective for Access 2007.

#	Objective
3.2	**Navigate among records** • Move to a specific record • Move to the first or last record

Views

Explanation

Access provides several views, such as Datasheet, Design, Pivot Table, and Pivot Chart, for working with tables.

Datasheet view displays data in a tabular format, containing rows and columns. Datasheet view helps you scroll through records and add, edit, or view data in a table.

If you want to change the design of a table by adding or changing field details, you can do it in Design view. *Design* view gives you complete control over the table's structure.

To switch between Datasheet view and Design view, use the View buttons on the Window frame, or the View button on the Datasheet ribbon.

Pivot Table view helps you analyze data. *Pivot Chart* view helps you display data graphically in Datasheet view.

Do it!

B-1: Discussing views

Questions and answers

1 When you want to add or edit data in a table, which view will you work with?

2 If you want to modify the structure of a table, which view will you use?

3 Which view will help you in analyzing data?

4 You want to present the analysis of sales data in a meeting. Which view will you use?

Datasheet view

Explanation

By default, tables open in Datasheet view, as shown in Exhibit 2-1. Each column is a field, and each row is a record. Use the navigation buttons and scrollbars to scroll through the table. You can scroll to the left or to the right of the window by using the horizontal scrollbar. You can scroll up and down by using the vertical scrollbar.

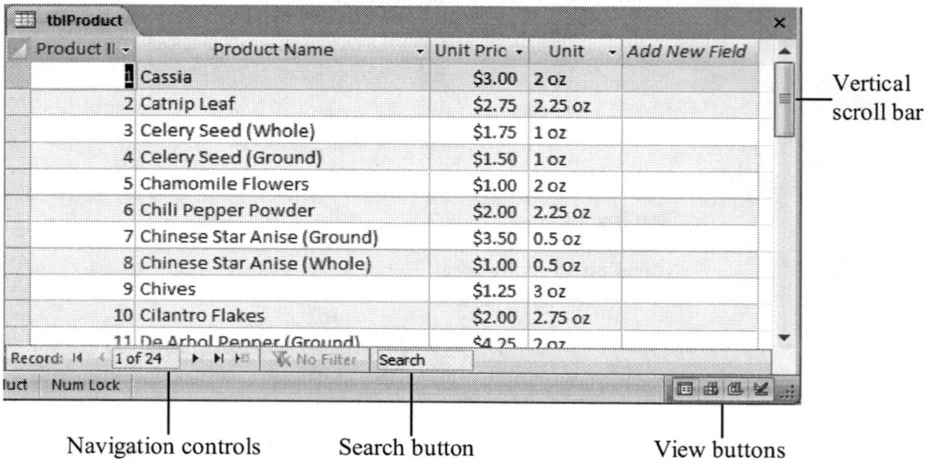

Exhibit 2-1: The tblProduct table in Datasheet view

Do it!

B-2: Examining a table in Datasheet view

Here's how	Here's why
1 Open AccessBasics	(Click the Office Button and choose Open.) From the current unit folder.
2 In the Navigation Pane, double-click **tblProduct**	(To open the tblProduct window, shown in Exhibit 2-1.) The tblProduct table is shown in Datasheet view. Datasheet appears as a contextual tab in the Ribbon.
3 Observe the fields in the table	Each column in the table represents a field. The fields are Product ID, Product Name, Unit Price, and Unit. You can add a new field by adding data under Add New Field.
Observe the records in the table	Each row in the table represents a record. There are 24 records in the table. You can add, edit, or delete records in Datasheet view.
Observe the lower-left area of the Datasheet window	In this area, "1 of 24" appears, indicating that the first record is now active and that there are 24 records in the table.

Navigating in a table

Explanation

In Datasheet view, you can navigate in a table by using the navigation buttons, as shown in Exhibit 2-2. These are located at the bottom of the Datasheet view window.

Exhibit 2-2: The navigation buttons and the record number box in Datasheet view

The following table describes the navigation buttons and the record number box.

Item	Description
	First record in the table
	Previous record
	The current active record in the table
	Next record
	Last record
	New (blank) record

Using the record selector

You can also navigate through the records and select specific records by using the *record selector*, which points to the currently active record and indicates its status. The record selector is the small box to the left of each record in a table. If you click in this box, the record next to it is highlighted, making it the active record.

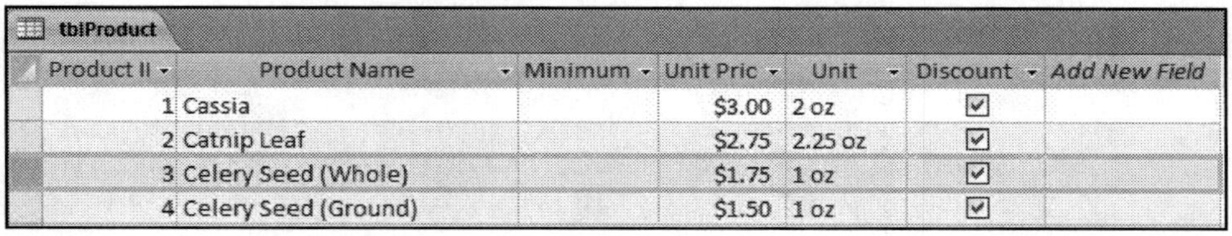
tblProduct

Product II	Product Name	Minimum	Unit Pric	Unit	Discount	Add New Field
1	Cassia		$3.00	2 oz	☑	
2	Catnip Leaf		$2.75	2.25 oz	☑	
3	Celery Seed (Whole)		$1.75	1 oz	☑	
4	Celery Seed (Ground)		$1.50	1 oz	☑	

Exhibit 2-3: A table with a selected record

The icon for the record selector changes based on the status of the record. When you click on a specific field in a record, both the record selector and the field name are highlighted in orange. The following table explains the different icons for the record selector:

Icon	Description
	Indicates that you are in the process of editing the record but have not yet saved it.
	Indicates that you can enter data for a new record.

Do it!

B-3: Navigating in a table in Datasheet view

Here's how	Here's why
1 Verify that the tblProduct table is open in Datasheet view	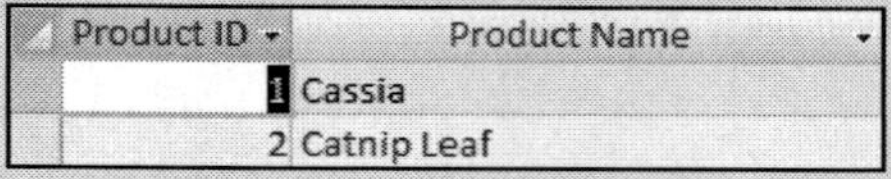 The record selector is highlighted on the left side of the data value 1.
2 Observe the record number box	 (At the bottom of the Datasheet view window.) It indicates that record 1 is the active record.
Click 	(The Next record button is at the bottom of the Datasheet window.) To move to the next record. The record selector moves to the left side of 2.
Observe the record number box	The record number box now reads 2 of 24.
3 Click 	(To move to the previous record.) The record selector is positioned to the left of the first row.
4 Click 	(To move to the last record.) The record selector is now next to the twenty-fourth record. Note that the record number is not the same as the product ID number.
5 Click 	To move to the first record.
Edit the record number box to read **5**	You'll move to the fifth record.
Press ENTER	The record selector is next to the fifth record.
6 Click 	To add a new record.
7 In the Product Name field of the new record, enter **Ancho Pepper (Ground)**	The value in the Product ID field automatically changes to 35. This occurs because the Product ID field is set to a numeric data type that will automatically increment by one each time you add a record.
Observe the record selector	It takes the shape of a pencil, indicating that you are in the process of editing a record.
Press TAB	To move to the next cell.

8	In the Unit Price field, enter **12.75**	Access 2007 inserts the $ automatically, because this field is formatted to display values as currency.
	Press TAB	To move to the next cell.
	In the Unit field, enter **2 oz**	
9	Press TAB twice	(To move to the next record.) Changes to a record are saved automatically when you move to a different record or close the table.

Design view

Explanation

The design of a table includes field names, the type of data each field stores, the field size, and the manner in which field values appear in the table. When you want to specify the properties of a field, such as Field Name and Data Type, you use Design view. In this view, the window is split into top and bottom panes, as shown in Exhibit 2-4.

If an object is already opened, you can switch to Design view by clicking Design View at the bottom right of the window frame, or by clicking View on the Datasheet ribbon and choosing Table Design. You can also right-click the object's tab and choose Design view from the context menu. If the object is not open, you can open it directly to Design view by right-clicking the object name in the Navigation Pane and choosing Design View.

The upper pane displays the design of the table in the following terms:

- **Field Name**—The name of each field.
- **Data Type**—The type of data stored in each field. For example, the Text data type stores text values, and Number data type stores numbers.
- **Description**—Explanation of the field's purpose.

The lower pane is the Field Properties pane. Here, you can see the properties, or attributes, of each field, including Field Size, Format, and Caption. The Format property specifies the way the data should appear in the table. The Caption property helps you specify titles for fields. These captions appear as field headings in the Datasheet view of the table. If you don't specify captions for the fields, the field names appear as the field headings. The other field properties vary depending on the data type of the field.

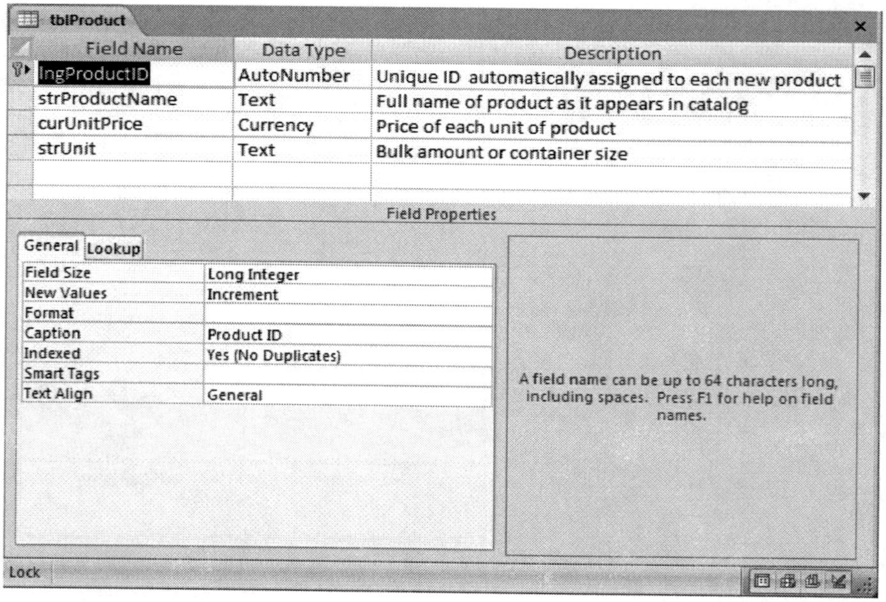

Exhibit 2-4: The tblProduct table in Design view

Do it!

B-4: Examining a table in Design view

Here's how	Here's why
1 Click 	(The View buttons are on the bottom right side of the Access window.) To switch to Design view.
2 Observe the window	The tblProduct window appears in Design view, as shown in Exhibit 2-4.
3 Observe the Field Name column	The Field Name column lists the fields in the table: lngProductID, strProductName, curUnitPrice, and strUnit. The corresponding field headings in Datasheet view are Product ID, Product Name, Unit Price, and Unit.
4 Observe the Data Type column	The data type for lngProductID is AutoNumber; the data type for strProductName and strUnit is Text; and for curUnitPrice it is Currency.
5 Observe the Description column	Each field has a description.
6 Observe the Field Properties pane	This pane shows the field properties specific to different data types. Exhibit 2-4 shows the properties of the lngProductID field.
7 Close the table window	Click the close button in the upper right.
8 Close the database	Click the Office Button and choose Close Database.

Topic C: Creating tables

This topic covers the following Microsoft Certified Application Specialist exam objectives for Access 2007.

#	Objective
1.1.1	**Define table fields** • Identify fields appropriate for Boolean operators
1.1.2	**Define appropriate table field data types for fields in each table** • Select a text or number field for the appropriate situation • Select the correct number type • When to use currency versus number • When to use a memo field • Multi-value fields
1.3.1	**Define and modify primary keys** • Default AutoNumber key • Define a data field as the primary key
1.3.2	**Define and modify multi-field primary keys**
2.2.1	**Create custom tables in Design view**
2.2.2	**Create tables by copying the structure of other tables**
2.2.3	**Create tables from templates**
2.3.3	**Rename tables**
2.3.4	**Delete tables**
2.4.1	**Create commonly used fields** • Text fields • Number fields • Date/Time fields • Currency fields • AutoNumber fields • Yes/No fields • Memo fields
3.1	**Enter, edit, and delete records** • Edit records

Creating a table

Explanation

Tables are the heart of the database. This is where the data is stored. Most other objects—forms, queries, and reports—are based on the data found in tables.

After creating a database, you need to create tables in which to store the data. By default, Access creates one new blank table when you create a new database. You can create an additional table in any of the following ways:

- By using the table templates
- By using Design view
- By using Datasheet view
- By copying the structure of an existing table

After creating a table, you can add fields to it and set the primary key. A *primary key* is a field that uniquely identifies each record in a table. For example, you can use a separate number for each retailer; these numbers will identify the retailers uniquely. After you've created a table by using the table templates, you can modify field names, data types, field sizes, or other field properties in Design view.

When you create a table in datasheet view, the table opens with nondescript field names and no set data types. While this might be acceptable for some quick tasks, you will probably want to start with a template or custom-designed table in Design view.

Using the table templates

Like the database templates, table templates provide you with a starting point, a rough draft that you can then modify to suit your needs.

To create a table by using table templates:

1. Open the database in which you want to create a table.
2. Activate the Create tab.
3. In the Tables group, click Table Templates and select an appropriate template.
4. To rename columns, right-click on the field name and choose Rename Column.
5. To delete a column, right-click in the field name and choose Delete Column.
6. To add a new column, right-click Add New Field and choose Insert Column, then rename the new column.
7. To modify the table in more detail, use switch to Design view.
8. To rename the table, close it then right-click the table name and choose Rename.

Exhibit 2-5: The fields in the table created from the Events template

Do it!

C-1: Creating a table by using the table templates

Here's how	Here's why
1 Open CreateDatabase	Click the Office Button and choose Open. Then navigate to the current unit folder and select the file.
2 Activate the **Create** tab	
3 In the Tables group, click **Table Templates** and select **Events**	A new table opens in datasheet view with fields shown in Exhibit 2-5.
4 Right click the field name **Title** and choose **Rename Column**	You'll rename and add columns to make this table suit your needs.
Edit the field name to read **Course**	
5 Right click **Add New Field** and choose **Insert Column**	(At the top of the last field.) A new column named Field1 appears.
Rename the new field **Room**	Right-click the field name and choose Rename Column.
6 Switch to Design view	(Right-click the table tab and choose Design View.) The Save As dialog box appears. Access prompts you to save the changes you have made before switching the view.
Click **OK**	To save this table with its default name, Table1, and switch to Design view.
Observe the fields and data types	Note that an AutoNumber ID field is added as a unique identifier and is set as the primary key.
7 Close the table	Right-click the table tab and choose Close.
8 In the Navigation Pane, right-click the new table name and choose **Rename**.	
Edit the name to read **Seminars** and press ENTER	

Creating tables in Design view

Explanation

To create a table in Design view:

1. Open the database in which you want to create the table.
2. Activate the Create tab.
3. Click the Table Design button in the Tables group to open a new table in Design view.

You can also create a new table—with or without a template—in Datasheet view and then switch to Design view.

You can then enter the necessary information, such as adding a field name and description in the Field and Description columns. Another column, Data Type, contains a drop-down arrow that you can use to select a data type from the list.

Design view contains a row selector, which indicates the active field with a black triangle, as shown in Exhibit 2-6. The lower pane is the Field Properties pane, which contains two tabs: General and Lookup. Use the General tab to set field properties, such as the size of a field. Use the Lookup tab to modify field properties, such as the appearance of a field in a table.

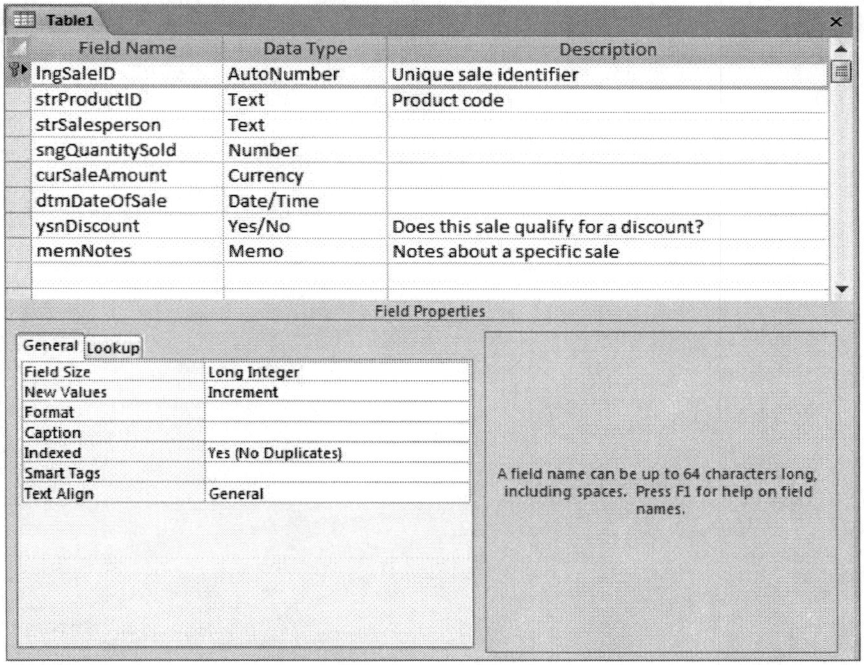

Exhibit 2-6: A new table in Design view

Do it!

C-2: Creating a table in Design view

Here's how	Here's why
1 Activate the Create tab	You'll create a table in this database by using Design view.
2 Click **Table Design**	 (In the Tables group.) To open a new table in Design view.
3 Observe the table title	The title is Table1.
Observe the upper pane of the window	The highlighted row selector is positioned to the left of the first record.
Observe the Field Properties pane	This pane has two tabs: General and Lookup. By default, the General tab is activated.

Adding fields

Explanation

You can use various data types, such as text or number, depending on the type of data the field should store. For example, if you want to store addresses or product codes that contain characters, numbers, or a combination of both, you can choose the Text data type.

1 In Design view, place the insertion point in the Field Name column, and enter a name for the field.
2 Press Tab to move to the Data Type column. Click the drop-down arrow, and select Text from the Data Type list.
3 Press Tab to move to the Description column. Enter a description of the field.

The following table describes some of the data types, along with the size and type of data they can store:

Data type	Size	Type of data stored
Text	Up to 255 characters.	Text information or combinations of text and numbers, such as an address, name, or phone number.
Number	Several sizes available to store numbers with varying degrees of precision.	Numeric information used in calculations.
Date/Time	Accommodates dates and time across thousands of years.	Dates and times, such as 10/23/2007 2:00:00 PM.
Currency	Up to 15 digits to the left of the decimal point and 4 digits to the right.	Monetary values, such as $5.00.
Yes/No	Size controlled by Access.	Stores one of two values: Yes or No.
Memo	Up to 65,535 characters.	Long text such as comments or notes.
AutoNumber	N/A	A number that increments automatically with each new record. It can be used to provide a unique ID for a record, and is often used for primary keys.
OLE object	Up to 2 GB of data.	Images, documents, graphs, and other objects.
Hyperlink	Up to 1 GB of data.	Internet or LAN addresses.
Attachment		Images, workbook files, documents, and other types of files. Unlike OLE objects, attached files can be viewed and edited, and require less storage space.
Lookup	N/A	Links to lists in other tables, or a list of user-defined values. Also called multi-value field.

The Number data type provides field size settings. Field sizes that can accommodate large or complex numbers use more storage space than field sizes for smaller numbers. You should choose field sizes that are appropriate for the type of numeric data to be stored. If the field size is too small, the data cannot be stored. If it is too large, the database will grow unnecessarily large.

Field size	Description	Decimals	Size
Byte	Whole numbers from 0 to 255.	None	1 byte
Integer	Whole numbers from –32,68 to 32,767.	None	2
Long Integer	(The default.) Whole numbers from –2,147,483,648 to 2,147,483,647.	None	4
Single	Decimal values from -3.4 x 10^{38} to 3.4 x 10^{38}	0-7	4
Double	Decimal values from -1.797 x 10^{308} to 1.797 x 10^{308}	0-15	8
Decimal	Decimal values from -10^{28} to 10^{28}	0-28	12
Replication ID	A Globally Unique Identifier (GUID) used to identify database objects when replicating databases.	N/A	16

The default size for a text field is 50 characters. However, you can change the field size by using the General tab of the Field Properties pane. You can't assign the Text data type to a field if you want to enter a date in it or perform calculations. For dates or numerals, you assign data types such as Date/Time or Number.

The Memo data type stores long text data, which might include characters and numbers. For example, a Memo field could be used to store notes on a specific sale.

To add fields of any data type to your table, enter the field name in the Field Name column and select the data type from the Data Type list.

Boolean operations

When choosing a data type for a field, consider the way the field will be used in database operations. If the field will need to support searches or comparisons, be sure to use a data type that supports Boolean operators such as `and`, `or`, `not`; and comparison operators such as `equal`, `not equal`, `less than`, etc. The data types that lend themselves most easily to Boolean operations include:

- Text
- Number
- Date/Time
- Currency
- Yes/No
- AutoNumber

Do it!

C-3: Adding fields and descriptions to a table

Here's how	Here's why
1 In the Field Name column, enter **lngSaleID**	This is the name of the first field in the table.
Press TAB	To move to the Data Type column. You'll see a drop-down arrow.
2 Click the drop-down arrow	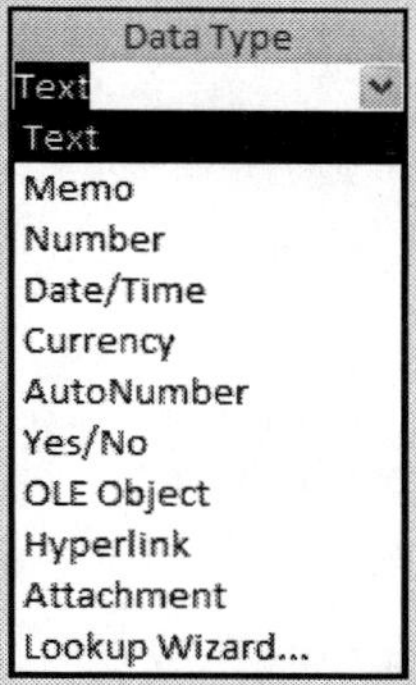 To display the Data Type list. By default, Text is selected. You'll change the Data Type for this field.
From the Data Type list, select **AutoNumber**	This will be the data type for the lngSaleID field. Each time a record is added to the table, this field will increment automatically.
Press TAB	To move to the Description column.
In the Description column, enter **Unique sale identifier**	
3 Press TAB	To enter the second field. The row selector moves to the next field row.
In the Field Name column, enter **strProductID**	
Press TAB	To move to the Data Type column. Text is selected as the data type.
4 Press TAB	To accept Text as the data type and move to the Description column. If the Product ID field will be used in searches or comparisons, then making this a text field will help to ensure that Boolean operations execute efficiently.
In the Description column, enter **Product code**	

5	Press TAB	To enter the third field. The row selector moves to the next field row.
	Enter **strSalesperson**	This is the name of the third field.
	Press TAB	To move to the Data Type column. Text is selected as the data type.
6	In the Field Name column, place the insertion point in the third row	You'll skip the descriptions and add another field to the table.
	Enter **sngQuantitySold**	This is the name of the fourth field.
	Press TAB	You'll select a data type for the sngQuantitySold field.
	From Data Type list, select **Number**	This field will store the number of units (pounds or kg) sold, rather than the sales amount in dollars. A number field is required rather than a currency field.
7	In the Field Properties pane at the bottom of the window, click beside **Long Integer**	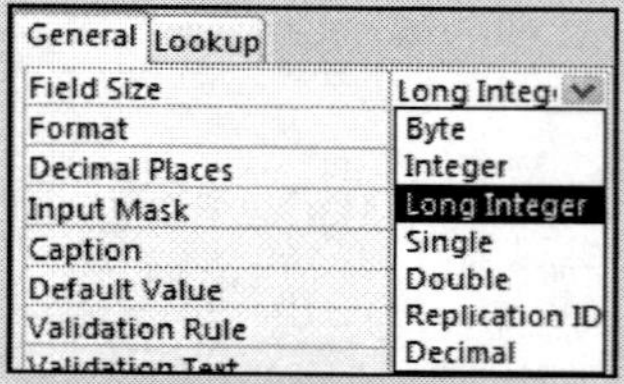 The list of Field Sizes displays.
	Observe the Field Sizes	You'll keep Long Integer as the field size, because decimal values are not required, and a large customer might conceivably order more than 32,767 units of an item.
8	Add the field **curSaleAmount**	This field will store the amount of the sale.
	From the Data Type list, select **Currency**	This will be the data type for the curSaleAmount field.
9	Add the field **dtmDateOfSale**	This field will store the date on which a sale was made.
	From Data Type list, select **Date/Time**	This will be the data type for the dtmDateOfSale field.
10	Add the field **ysnDiscount**	This field will store the status of the availability of discounts for specific products.
	From Data Type list, select **Yes/No**	This will be the data type for the Discount field.
	In the Description field, enter **Does this sale qualify for a discount?**	

11 Add the field **memNotes**	This will be the sixth field. It will store details about sales.
From the Data Type list, select **Memo**	Notes about a sale might require more than the 255 characters available in an ordinary Text field.
In the Description column, enter **Notes about a specific sale**	

Setting the primary key for a table

Explanation

Sometimes, you might find that two records in a table have the same value, making it difficult to differentiate between them. For example, a field called strSalesperson could store duplicate values if two or more salespeople have the same name. This would make this field a poor choice for the primary key, which should be a unique identifier for each record in the database. A better choice might be an Autonumber ID field.

To set a field as a primary key, do either of the following:

- Select the field and click Primary Key on the Design tab.
- Right-click the field row, and select Primary Key from the shortcut menu.

Do it!

C-4: Setting the primary key

Here's how	Here's why
1 In the Field Name column, place the insertion point in the third row	You'll set the strSalesperson as the primary key.
2 Click **Primary Key**	 (The Primary Key button is on the Design ribbon.) A key icon appears to the left of strSalesperson to show that it is now the primary key. The strSalesperson field is not a good choice for primary key, because the values in this field can repeat within the database.
3 In the Field Name column, place the insertion point in the first row	You'll set the lngSaleID, the default Autonumber field, as the primary key instead.
4 Click **Primary Key**	A key icon appears to the left of lngSaleID to show that it is now the primary key. At this point, the view should resemble Exhibit 2-6.

Saving tables

Explanation

After you have completed the table design, you need to save it. You can save a table by clicking the Office Button and choosing Save As or Save. By choosing Save As, you can save a table with a different name. You need to provide a name for the table before saving it for the first time. You can also save a table by right-clicking the table tab and choosing Save.

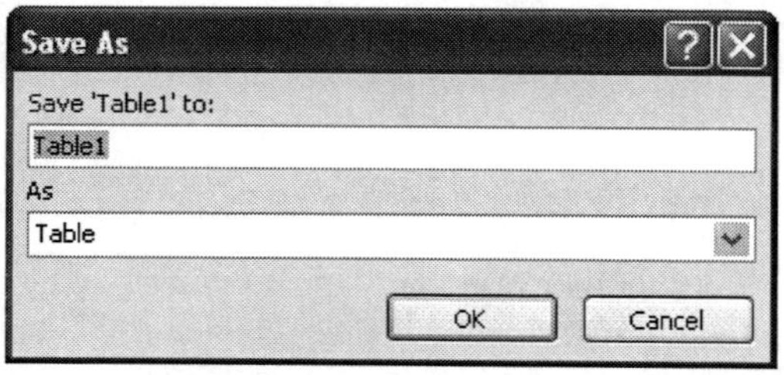

Exhibit 2-7: The Save As dialog box

Do it!

C-5: Saving the table

Here's how	Here's why
1 Click 	To display the File menu.
Choose **Save As**	To open the Save As dialog box, as shown in Exhibit 2-7.
2 Edit the Save Table 'Table1' To box to read **tblSales**	You'll save the table as tblSales.
In the As list, verify that Table is selected	
Click **OK**	(To save the table.) The table name appears in the Navigation Pane.

Adding records

Explanation

After you create and save a table, you can enter data in it. To do so, you need to open the table in Datasheet view. When you type data into a record, Access automatically saves the record when you move the insertion point out of that record.

There are three ways to enter data in a table:

- Click the new record navigation button.
- Place the insertion point in the row under the first field heading, and enter data.

Do it!

C-6: Adding a record

Here's how	Here's why
1 Switch to Datasheet view	You'll add a record to the table.
2 In the strProductID column, enter **101**	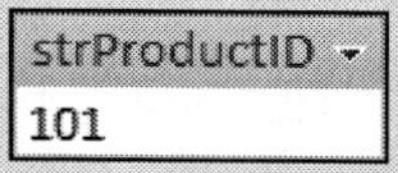 This is the product ID for the first product.
Observe the lngSaleID field	When you entered data in this record, the lngSaleID field automatically inserted a 1, because this is an Autonumber field.
3 Press TAB	To move to the next field.
4 In the strSalesperson column, enter **Bill MacArthur**	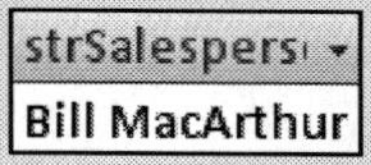 This is the salesperson's name for the first record.
5 Point to the line between the second and third field names	You'll resize the columns to see the whole field name.
Drag the border as indicated	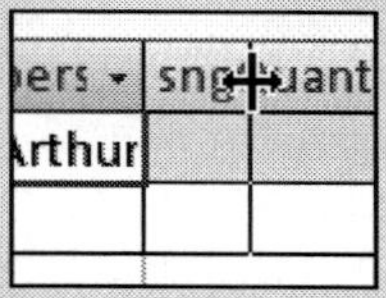
6 Resize the other columns as necessary	So you can see the whole field names.
7 Edit the sngQuantitySold column to read **30**	
8 Edit the curSaleAmount column to read **625.5**	 The format changes when you leave the field. The default format is Auto, which displays a dollar sign and two decimal places.

9	In the dtmDateOfSale column, enter **12/13/06**	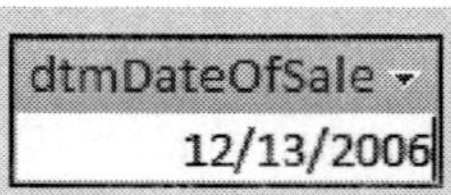 The format changes to show a four-digit year when you leave the field. The default format is mm/dd/yyyy.
10	In the ysnDiscount column, check as shown	 There are only two possible values for a yes/no field. This is also called true/false or Boolean.
11	In the memNotes column, enter **Purchase order no. 3710**	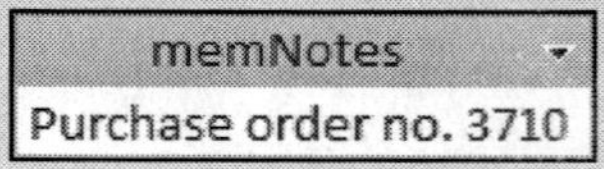 Resize the column to see all of this.
12	Right-click the table tab and choose **Close**	A message box prompts you to save changes.
	Click **Yes**	To close the table and save the changes to the layout. The data itself is saved as you leave each field.

Copying and modifying tables

Explanation

You can create a new table by copying the structure of an existing table.

To copy a table:

1. In the Navigation Pane, right-click the table to be copied and choose Copy.
2. Right-click any blank space within the Navigation Pane and choose Paste. The Paste Table As dialog box appears, as shown in Exhibit 2-8.
3. Edit the Table Name field to give the table a new name.
4. In the Paste Options, select Structure Only.
5. Click OK.

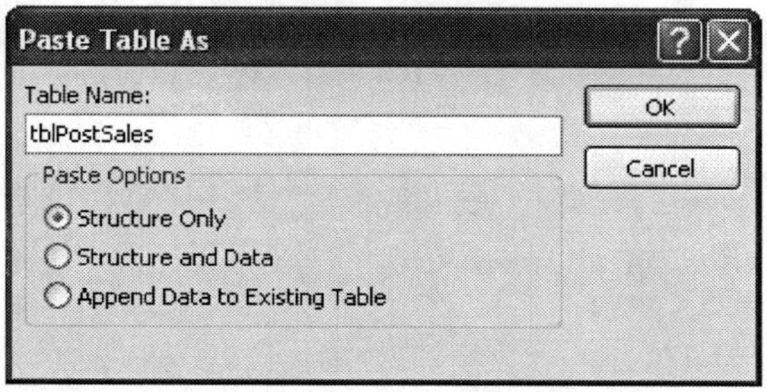

Exhibit 2-8: The Paste Table As dialog box

Renaming and deleting tables

When you right-click a table in the Navigation Pane, the shortcut menu appears. You can use the shortcut menu for many operations, including renaming and deleting a table.

Do it!

C-7: Copying, modifying, and deleting a table

Here's how	Here's why
1 In the Navigation Pane, right-click tblSales	The shortcut menu appears. You'll create a new table by copying a table's structure.
Choose **Copy**	To copy tblSales. The shortcut menu closes.
2 Point to a blank area of the Navigation Pane and right-click	The shortcut menu appears.
Choose **Paste**	The Paste Table As dialog box appears.
3 Edit the Table Name to read **tblPostSales**	 To name the new table.
4 Under Paste Options, select **Structure Only**	 To copy only the table structure to the new table.
Click **OK**	To close the dialog box and create the new table. The new table appears in the Navigation Pane.
5 Open tblPostSales in Design View	Right-click the table and choose Design View.
Observe the fields	The structure of this table is identical to tblSales.
6 Switch to Datasheet View	(Right-click the table tab and choose Datasheet View.) The table is empty of data, because only the structure was copied.
Close tblPostSales	
7 Right-click tblPostSales and choose Rename	You'll rename the table. The table name becomes editable.
Edit the table name to read **discard**	
8 Right-click the table and choose **Delete**	You'll remove this table from the database. The Microsoft Office Access dialog box appears.
Click **Yes**	To confirm that you want to delete the table. The table is removed from the Navigation Pane.
Close the database	

Setting two primary keys for a table

Explanation

You can define two fields as the primary key for a table. This type of primary key is called a composite key. It is also called a compound key or a multi-field key.

Composite keys are typically used if a table has no single field (with a set of unique values) that can serve as the primary key. However, there may be two or more fields which, when combined, create a unique value. These fields can be defined as the composite key.

To define two or more fields as a composite key:

1. Open the table in Design View.
2. Press and hold Ctrl.
3. Select the first row that will be part of the composite key.
4. Select the next row or rows that will be part of the composite key.
5. Right-click the last row you selected and choose Primary Key.
6. Release the Ctrl key.

A key icon appears beside each row that is part of the composite key, as shown in Exhibit 2-9.

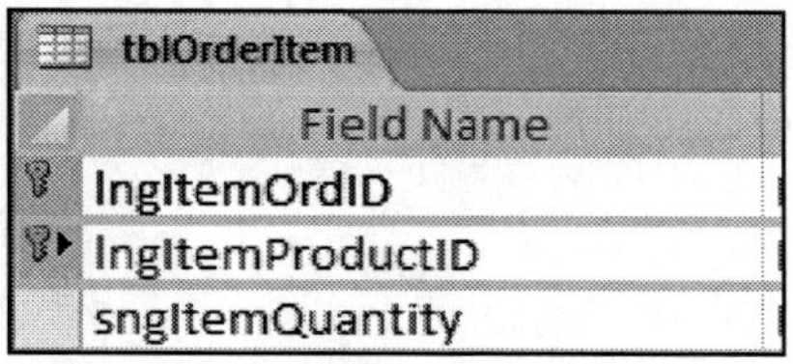

Exhibit 2-9: A table with a composite key

Do it!

C-8: Creating a composite key

Here's how	Here's why
1 Open CompositeKey	(Click the Office button, choose Open, and select CompositeKey.)
2 Open **tblOrderItem**	You'll create a composite key for this table.
Observe the Order ID field	There are multiple occurrences of each Order ID. This field cannot be used as the primary key, because the fields are not unique.
Observe the Product field	This field also has repeated values, and cannot be used as the primary key. However, each combination of Order ID and Product provides a unique value.
3 Switch to Design View	Right-click the table tab and select Design View.
Observe the fields in the database	There is no key icon in the far left column. This table has no primary key.
4 Select the first row	(If necessary.) Click the column to the left of lngItemOrdID.
Press and hold CTRL	Hold this key during the next two steps.
Select the second row	Click the column to the left of lngItemProductID.
5 Click **Primary Key**	(In the Design tab.) To make both fields the primary key.
6 Observe the table	A key icon appears in the column beside each row. Both fields comprise the primary key, as shown in Exhibit 2-9.
7 Close the table	Right-click the table tab and select Close. The Microsoft Office Access dialog box appears, prompting you to save changes.
Click **Yes**	To save the changes.
Close the database	

Unit summary: Databases and tables

Topic A

In this topic, you learned how to **plan a database**. You learned the importance of following the **naming rules** while creating a database and its objects. You also learned how to create a database by using the **Database Templates**. In addition, you learned how to **create a blank database**. Finally, you learned that you have more flexibility when creating a blank database.

Topic B

In this topic, you learned how to use various views, such as **Design** and **Datasheet**. You learned that you can use Datasheet view to scroll through records, and use Design view to modify a table's design. You also learned how to **examine** a **table** in Datasheet view and in Design view.

Topic C

In this topic, you learned how to create a table by using the **Table Templates** and how to modify a table in Design view. In addition, you learned how to create a table in **Design view**. You also learned how to add **Text, Number**, **Date/Time**, **Yes/No**, and **Memo fields** to a new table. You also learned how to add an **Autonumber** field, how to set the **primary key** in Design view, and how to **save** a table. Next, you learned how to **add a record** to a table. Then, you learned how to create a table by **copying the structure** of another table. You learned how to **rename** and **delete** tables. Finally, you learned how to define a **composite key** for a table.

Review questions

1 Why would you use Database Templates to create a database?

2 What is the advantage of creating a database manually?

3 Which of the following views displays data in a tabular format containing rows and columns?

A Design view

B Datasheet view

C Chart view

D Pivot Table view

4 Which view is used to add field details?

5 In Datasheet view, how do you move between records?

6 Which view is used to enter data in a table?

Independent practice activity

In this activity, you'll plan and create a database. You'll create a table for this database by using a template. Next, you'll add records and set the primary key. Finally, you'll add data and save the table and database.

1 Plan and design a database for storing information about customers who place orders for different products. The database should have a minimum of two tables.

2 Create a new blank database with a name of your choice.

3 Close the default table. Delete it if necessary. (*Hint*: Right-click the table name and choose Delete.)

4 Create a table by using table templates using a template of your choice. (*Hint*: Activate the Create tab to start.)

5 Change and add fields to suit your intended purpose. (*Hint*: Invent one.)

6 Save and close the table.

7 Create a table in Design view, set the primary key, and add the fields shown in Exhibit 2-10.

8 Save the table as tblCustomerOrder.

9 Enter data in tblCustomerOrder as shown in Exhibit 2-11. Adjust column width as necessary.

10 Save and close the table.

11 Close the database.

Field Name	Data Type	Description
lngOrderNo	AutoNumber	Order number, automatically generated by Access
strProductID	Text	Product identification number
dtmOrderDate	Date/Time	Date the order was placed
strCustomer	Text	Name of customer who placed the order
lngOrderQuantity	Number	Quantity of product ordered by customer
ysnDispatched	Yes/No	If the order has already dispatched

Exhibit 2-10: The tblCustomerOrder table in Design view after Step 7

lngOrderNo	strProductID	dtmOrderDate	strCustomer	lngOrderQuantity	ysnDispatched
1	1	1/2/2007	Rebecca Austin	250	☑
2	2	2/2/2007	Annie Philips	367	☐
3	3	12/3/2007	Julie Stone	234	☐

Exhibit 2-11: The records in the tblCustomerOrder table after Step 9

Unit 3

Fields and records

Complete this unit, and you'll know how to:

A Modify the table design by modifying field names, inserting and deleting fields, moving fields, and using the attachment data type.

B Find and replace data in a table.

C Sort, filter, and delete records.

Topic A: Changing the design of a table

This topic covers the following Microsoft Certified Application Specialist exam objectives for Access 2007.

#	Objective
2.3.5	**Summarize table data by adding a Total row**
2.4.2	**Modify field properties** • Enter captions
2.4.4	**Create and modify attachment fields** • Multiple attachments • Assign attachment data type to a field
3.4	**Attach documents to and detach from records** • Attach multiple attachments to records • Attach files to records • Detach attachments from records • Export attachments • Navigate attachments

Effective field names

Explanation

After you create a table, you can edit its design. You can delete fields, insert new fields, change field names, or change the order in which fields appear. You make these modifications in Design view.

It will be easier for you and for others to use your database if you give each field a name that reflects its purpose. For example, the field name ProductName is easier to understand than the field name Pname.

To make the field names clear and readable, you should use a combination of uppercase and lowercase letters. Exhibit 3-1 shows a table with field names that are not very meaningful.

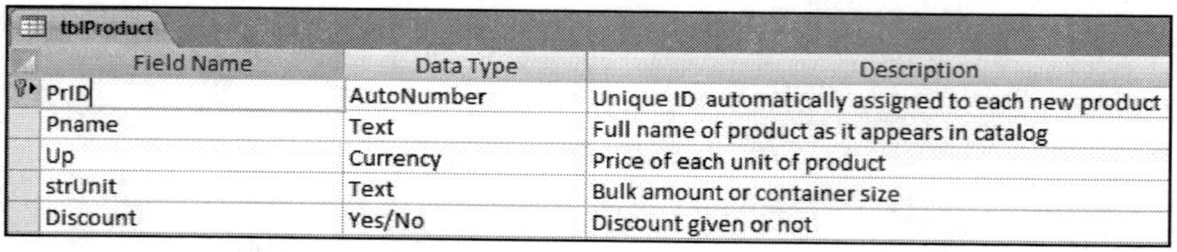

tblProduct

Field Name	Data Type	Description
PrID	AutoNumber	Unique ID automatically assigned to each new product
Pname	Text	Full name of product as it appears in catalog
Up	Currency	Price of each unit of product
strUnit	Text	Bulk amount or container size
Discount	Yes/No	Discount given or not

Exhibit 3-1: A table with uninformative field names

Ideally, the name of a field should be self-explanatory. You can change any field name in Design view. Changing the field name does not affect the existing data in the table.

It's also helpful if you use consistent naming conventions and names that reflect both the field's data type and its purpose. It is common convention to begin a field name with a lower-case abbreviation of the data type, followed by capitalized descriptive words. The following table shows some examples:

Data type	Purpose	Field name
Text (string)	Employee last name	strEmpLastName
Memo	Product description	memItemDesc
Number (long integer)	Employee number	lngEmpID
Date	Shipping date	dtmShipDate
Currency	Product cost	curProductCost
Hyperlink	Supplier Web site	hypSupplierHome

Do it!

A-1: Modifying field names

Here's how	Here's why
1 Open WorkingWithRecords	(Click File, Open, and select WorkingWithRecords from the current unit folder, and then click Open.)
2 In the Navigation Pane, right-click **tblProduct** and choose **Design View**	(To open the table in Design view.) You'll analyze the design of this table.
3 Under the Field Name column, observe the field names PrID and Pname	You'll change the field names to make them more self-explanatory.
4 Select **PrID**	(If necessary.) You'll change the name of the first field.
Enter **lngProductID**	This will be the new name for the first field. (lng stands for "long integer.")
5 Change the other field names as shown	Field Name lngProductID strProductName curUnitPrice strUnit ysnDiscount
6 Right-click the table tab and click **Save**	To update the table.

Deleting and inserting fields in a table

Explanation

After you create a table, you might find that you need to add or delete fields. You must first select a field to delete it or to insert a record over it.

Selecting a field

You can select a field by clicking its row selector, as shown in Exhibit 3-2. When you move the pointer over the row selector, it changes to an arrow. Clicking the row selector highlights the row with a thick border. You can now delete this field or insert a new field above it.

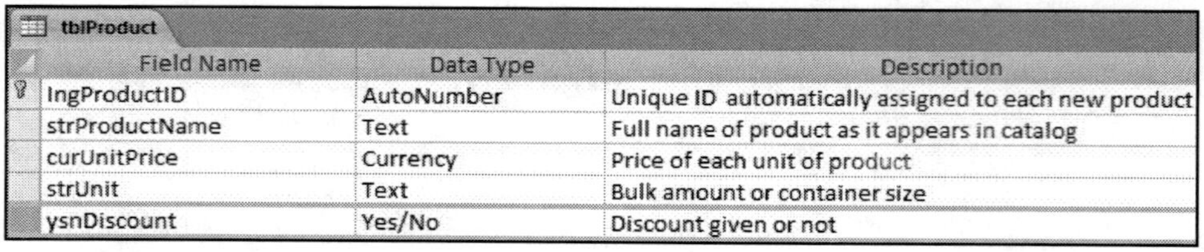

tblProduct

Field Name	Data Type	Description
lngProductID	AutoNumber	Unique ID automatically assigned to each new product
strProductName	Text	Full name of product as it appears in catalog
curUnitPrice	Currency	Price of each unit of product
strUnit	Text	Bulk amount or container size
ysnDiscount	Yes/No	Discount given or not

Exhibit 3-2: A table with the last field selected

Deleting a field

To delete a field in Design view, select the field and then either press the Delete key or click Delete Rows on the Design tab. For example, in the tblProduct table, if you want to delete the ysnDiscount field, first select the field, as shown in Exhibit 3-2, and then press Delete. Access prompts you to confirm the deletion if the field contains data or if the field is a primary key. Access will not prompt you if the field is empty.

Inserting a field

In Design view, you can insert a field either at the end of the table or above an existing field. To insert a field above an existing field, select the field above which you want to insert the new field, and click Insert Rows. To add a new field at the end, just enter a field name in the first empty row.

Captions

By default, the field name displays for each record at the top of its column in Datasheet view. But field names, while they contain useful information for the developer, are not always user-friendly for an end user. Therefore, for the benefit of the end user, you can enter a caption for a field. The caption displays in place of the field name in all views except for Design view. To enter a caption in Design view, select a field, then enter its caption on the General tab in the Field Properties pane at the bottom of Design view.

Do it!

A-2: Deleting and inserting fields

Here's how	Here's why
1 Click the row selector for the ysnDiscount field as shown	 To select the field. The pointer changes into a black arrow when it's over a row selector.
2 In the Tools group, click 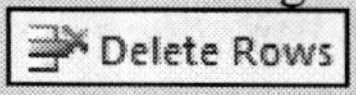	(On the Design tab.) A message box appears asking if you want to permanently delete the selected field and all its data.
Click **Yes**	To delete the ysnDiscount field from the table.
3 Select the **curUnitPrice** row	You'll insert a field above this field.
4 Click 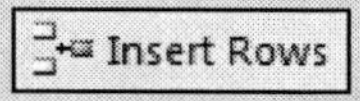	(A blank row appears above the field curUnitPrice.) The insertion point is in the first cell of the new row.
Under Field Name, in the inserted row, enter **sngMinQuantity**	(To specify the new field name.) This field stores data for the minimum quantity to be stored for each product.
Under Data Type, select **Number**	
Under Description, enter **Minimum quantity stored**	
5 In the Caption property, enter **Minimum**	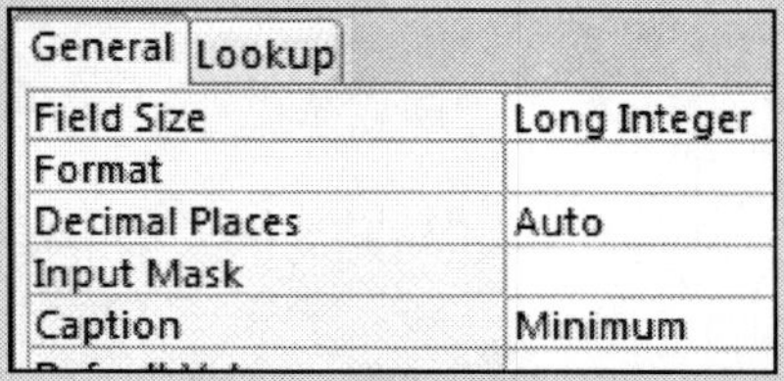 In the Field Properties pane, on the General tab.
6 Click 	(The Save button is on the Quick Access Toolbar, to the right of the Office Button.) To update the table. Update the table whenever you modify it.

Moving fields

Explanation

If you enter the field details in an unsuitable sequence when you create a table, you might want to rearrange the fields by moving the field rows in Design view.

To move a field row:

1. Select the field row by using the row selector.
2. Drag the row selector to its new place in the list. The pointer changes to an arrow with a box. When you drop the field, the field row in that position automatically shifts down to the next row.

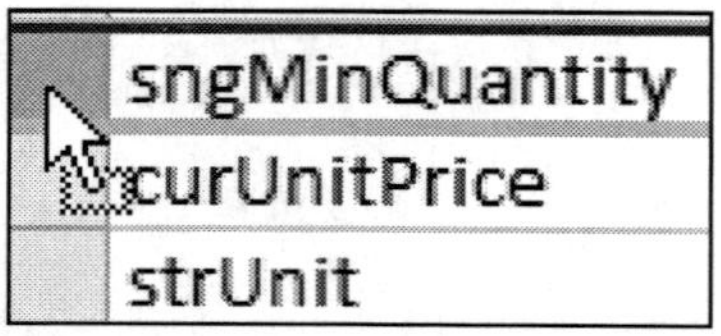

Exhibit 3-3: The pointer when moving a field

Do it!

A-3: Moving a field

Here's how	Here's why
1 Select the row for the field sngMinQuantity	(Click the row selector for the field sngMinQuantity.) You'll move this field below the field strUnit.
2 Drag the sngMinQuantity row selector to the row below strUnit	(As shown in Exhibit 3-3.) The mouse pointer changes to an arrow with a box, indicating that you can now drag the field to a new location. When you see a heavy black line below strUnit, you'll know you're moving the row to the correct position. The entire row for sngMinQuantity is moved here.
3 Update the table	Click the Save button, or right-click the table tab and choose Save.

The attachment data type

Explanation

The attachment data type can provide more detail to data in a table. You can use it to include documents, graphics, or other files as attachments to a field.

To use the attachment data type:

1. Open a table in Design view.
2. Add a field to house the attachment for a record.
3. Under Data Type, select Attachment.
4. Save the table.
5. Switch to Datasheet view.
6. Right-click the attachment field for the first record and choose Manage Attachments. The Attachments dialog box appears.
7. Click Add. The Choose File dialog box appears.
8. Select the desired file(s) and click Open.
9. Click OK to close the Attachments dialog box.

When you double-click the attachments field, the Attachments dialog box appears, as shown in Exhibit 3-4. You can then open, save, or remove any attached files.

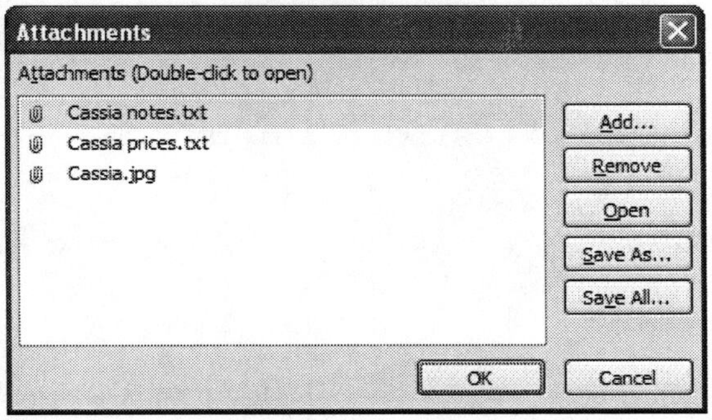

Exhibit 3-4: The Attachments dialog box

Do it!

A-4: Using the Attachment data type

Here's how	Here's why
1 Select the row below sngMinQuantity	You'll add an attachment type field to this table.
Under Field Name, enter **atchDetails**	(To specify the new field name.) This field will store an image file and a text file for each product.
Under Data Type, select **Attachment**	
Under Description, enter **Photos and descriptions of product**	
2 In the Caption prpperty, enter **Details**	In the Field Properties pane, on the General tab.
3 Update the table	You must update the table to switch views.
4 Switch to Datasheet view	
5 Observe the record for **Cassia**	The Details field displays a zero in parentheses. There are no files attached to this record.
6 Right-click within the Details field and choose **Manage Attachments...**	The Attachments dialog box appears.
Click **Add**	The Choose File dialog box appears.
Select **Cassia.jpg**	In the current unit folder.
Select **Cassia notes.txt** and **Cassia prices.txt**	Press the Crtl while clicking the files to select all.
7 Click **Open**	To close the Choose File dialog box. The three files appear in the Attachments dialog box.
8 Click **OK**	To close the Attachments dialog box and add the three files to the record. The Details field now displays a 3 in parentheses to indicate that this record has three attachments.
Double-click the field	The Attachments dialog box appears.
Double-click **Cassia.jpg**	The image displays in the computer's default viewer application.
Close the viewer	

9	Double-click **Cassia notes.txt**	The text displays in the computer's default text program.
	Close the text file	
10	Display **Cassia prices.txt**	The text in Cassia prices.txt is both redundant and out of date (the price has gone up.) You'll delete this attachment to avoid confusing other users.
	Close the text file	
11	Click **Remove**	(In the Attachments dialog box.) To delete the attachment. The file Cassia.jpg is now selected in the dialog box. You'll export this attached file.
12	Click **Save As...**	To open the Save Attachment dialog box. You'll export this attachment to a separate file.
	Edit the File name box to read **Cassia bark.jpg**	
	Click **Save**	To export the file.
	Click **OK**	To close the Attachments dialog box. The Details field now displays a 2 in parentheses.
13	Update and close the table	

Adding total rows

Explanation

You can add a total row at the bottom of a table to summarize its data. The fields in the total row can perform a variety of operations.

When you insert a Totals row, a Totals field appears at the bottom of each column in the table. For a numeric field, such as a Number or Currency data type, the total field can perform the following operations:

- Sum
- Average
- Count
- Maximum
- Minimum
- Standard Deviation
- Variance

If the field is a non-numeric field, such as a text or memo field, then the total at the bottom can perform a Count of the number of records.

Do it!

A-5: Adding a total row

	Here's how	Here's why
1	Open tblEmployee	You'll add a Totals row to this table.
	Scroll to the bottom of the table	So that you can see the last row.
	Click **Totals**	Σ Totals (The Totals button is in the Records group on the Home tab.) A Total row appears at the bottom of the table, below the New blank record row.
2	Click the **Total** field	(At the bottom of the Emp ID column.) A list arrow appears.
	Click the arrow	To display the list. Emp ID is an AutoNumber field, not a numeric field. The only options in the list are None and Count.
	Select **Count**	This field now displays the number of employees in this table.
3	Click the total field at the bottom of the Hire Date column and select **Minimum** from the list	The hire date of the first employee hired appears.
4	Display the average employee salary	Click the field at the bottom of the Earnings column. From the list, select Average.
5	Update and close the table	

Topic B: Finding and editing records

This topic covers the following Microsoft Certified Application Specialist exam objective for Access 2007.

#	Objective
3.3	**Find and replace data** • Find by using criteria • Find by using wildcards • Replace data

Finding and replacing values

Explanation

Scrolling through a large table to find specific records is not practical. Instead, you can use the Find feature to locate records that meet criteria you enter. You can also use Find to locate data values and replace them with different values.

If you accidentally delete or modify some values in a record when entering data, you can restore the original values without reentering the data by pressing Ctrl+Z or clicking Undo on the Quick Access Toolbar.

To search for a value in a field:

1. Place the insertion point on the first data value in the specified field.
2. Activate the Home tab (if necessary).
3. In the Find group, click Find.
4. Specify criteria in the Find and Replace dialog box for the values you want to find.

The Find and Replace dialog box, shown in Exhibit 3-5, contains two tabs: Find and Replace. In the Find tab, you can specify criteria for the value you want to find. In the Replace tab, you can specify a value with which you want to replace it.

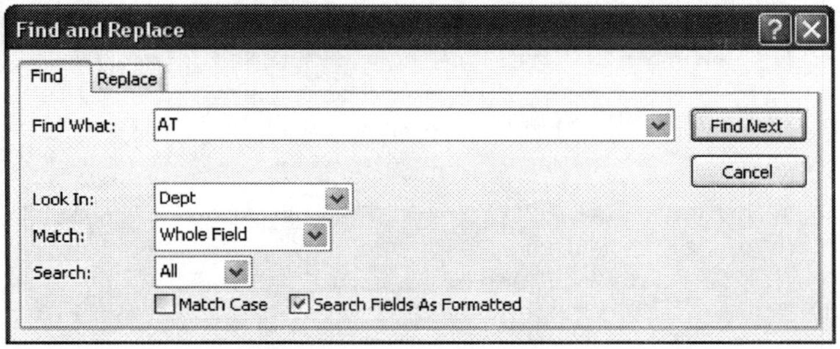

Exhibit 3-5: The Find and Replace dialog box

Wildcard searches

You can use wildcards to search for values in a field. A wildcard is a symbol that can represent any value, instead of a specific value. The asterisk (*) represents a string of any length, and the question mark (?) represents a single character. For example, searching a list of names for "Mar?" will return any four-letter string in which the first three characters are a match, such as Mark or Mary. But searching for "Mar*" will return strings of any length in which the first three characters match. In addition to Mark and Mary, it will return Marcus, Maria, and Martina.

Do it!

B-1: Finding and replacing a value

Here's how	Here's why
1 Open tblEmployee in datasheet view	Double-click the table name in the Navigation Pane. You'll find occurrences of the department code AT and replace them with AC.
2 Place the insertion point in the first data value in the Dept field	You'll search for a specific value in this field.
3 In the Find group, click **Find**	 (On the Home tab.) To open the Find and Replace dialog box. By default, the Find tab is activated.
In the Find What box, enter **AT**	To find this value in the Dept field.
In the Look In list, verify that **Dept** is selected	To specify that the value is to be searched for in the Dept field.
In the Match list, verify that **Whole Field** is selected	To specify that the search needs to be done with the entire field.
In the Search list, verify that **All** is selected	To specify that the entire table needs to be searched.
Click **Find Next**	The first occurrence of AT, corresponding to the employee Shannon Lee, is highlighted.
4 Activate the **Replace** tab	In the Find dialog box.
In the Replace With box, enter **AC**	

5	Click **Replace**	(To replace AT with AC.) The Dept entry for Shannon Lee changes to AC. The next occurrence of AT, corresponding to the employee Melissa James, is automatically highlighted.
	Click **Replace All**	To replace the remaining occurrences of AT without prompting for each. A message box appears asking you to confirm the replace operation.
	Click **Yes**	To confirm that you won't be able to undo this operation.
6	Place the insertion point in the first data value in the Emp HR# field	You'll search for a specific value in this field.
	In the Find What box, enter **04***	To find all values beginning with 04.
	Click **Find Next**	The first occurrence of a number beginning with 04, corresponding to the employee Shannon Lee, is highlighted.
	Click **Find Next**	The next occurrence of a number beginning with 04, corresponding to the employee Annie Philips, is highlighted.
7	Find the remaining records	Click Find Next to highlight each record that begins with 04. When all records have been found, the Microsoft Office Access dialog box displays.
	Click **OK**	To close the dialog box.
8	Click **Cancel**	To close the Find and Replace dialog box.
	Observe the values in the Dept field	All five instances of AT have been replaced with AC.

Undoing changes in a table

Explanation

If you accidentally delete or modify a record, you can press Ctrl+Z to restore the deleted or modified values. You can also press Undo on the Quick Access Toolbar. You can undo only the most recently changed value.

Do it!

B-2: Undoing changes

Here's how	Here's why
1 In the Earnings column, select the first data value	
Press DELETE	(To delete the value.) You'll check if this value can be restored.
2 Press CTRL+Z	To restore the deleted value.
3 Close the table	Do not save changes.

Topic C: Organizing records

This topic covers the following Microsoft Certified Application Specialist exam objectives for Access 2007.

#	Objective
3.1	**Enter, edit, and delete records** • Delete records
5.1.1	**Sort data within tables**
5.2.1	**Filter data within tables**
5.2.5	**Remove filters**

Sorting and filtering

Explanation

You can organize records by sorting, filtering, and deleting them. *Sorting* is the process of organizing records in a meaningful way so that you can retrieve data in an order of your choice. For example, if you want to view records in the ascending order of the last names of employees, you can sort the records based on the values in that field. You can sort records based on one or more fields.

Filtering is the process of temporarily isolating a subset of records that satisfy certain criteria you specify. For example, suppose that you want to delete or edit Human Resources department records in Datasheet view without navigating through the records of all the departments. To do this, you can filter the Human Resources department records to isolate them from the table containing the records of all the departments. You can also format and print the filtered records. Access provides several methods for filtering, such as Filter By Selection, Filter By Form, Filter Excluding Selection, and Advanced Filter/Sort.

When a column is sorted, a small arrow appears in the field heading. When a column is filtered, a small filter symbol (a funnel) appears in the column heading.

Sorting records by a single field in a table

Records in a table are automatically sorted based on the primary key field. However, you might want to sort the records based on a different field. The maximum number of characters for a sort field (or fields) is 255. You can sort in either ascending or descending order.

To sort a field in ascending order, select the field. In the Sort & Filter group, click Ascending or Descending.

You can also right-click the field and choose Sort A to Z or Sort Z to A from the shortcut menu. In ascending sort order, text values will be sorted alphabetically from A to Z, and date values will be sorted from the earliest to the latest. Number or currency values will be sorted from the lowest value to the highest.

Removing a Sort

To remove all sorts from a table, click Clear All Sorts in the Sort & Filter group. This button is enabled only if one or more columns are sorted.

Do it!

C-1: Sorting records by a single field

Here's how	Here's why
1 Open tblEmployee	
2 Select the Last Name column, or put the insertion point anywhere in that column	You'll sort records in the Last Name field in ascending order.
3 In the Sort & Filter group, click [A/Z↓]	(The Ascending key is on the Home tab.) The records are sorted in ascending order based on the Last Name field.
Observe the Last Name column heading	There is an arrow to the right of the field name, indicating that there is a sort on that column.
4 In the Sort & Filter group, click [Clear All Sorts]	The Clear All Sorts button returns the records to their original order. The arrow in the column heading is gone.

Sorting records by multiple fields in a table

Explanation

You can sort records based on more than one field by selecting the fields and clicking the Ascending or Descending button in the Sort & Filter group. The fields must be adjacent to each other in Datasheet view. The sort fields have precedence from left to right. For example, if you select the fields Dept and Hire Date from left to right, the records will be sorted based first on Dept and then on Hire Date.

Selecting and sorting multiple fields

To select two fields, click the field heading to select the first column. Then, hold down the Shift key and select the other adjacent column. Both columns will be highlighted, as shown in Exhibit 3-6. Then sort the fields as necessary.

You can select more fields while holding down the Shift key, but if you select non-adjacent columns, all the columns in between will also be selected. To sort on non-adjacent columns, just sort on one column and then the next; each sort will stay on the column until you clear it, with the most recent sort being the primary one.

You should also use this one-at-a-time method if you want to ensure which column is sorted first, second, third, etc. By default, when you select and sort on multiple columns, the left-most column is the primary sort column. For instance, in Exhibit 3-6, if you were to select and sort on both First Name and Last Name, the records would sort primarily on the first name, so Adam, Anna, and Annie would be first. To sort primarily on the last name, select and sort First Name, then select and sort Last Name.

First Name	Last Name	Dept	Hire Date	Earnings
Malcom	Pingault	SH	2/14/2001	$40,500.00
Shannon	Lee	AC	2/20/1998	$76,600.00
Melinda	McGregor	AD	5/5/2001	$30,200.00
James	Overmire	AD	9/19/1999	$87,000.00
Roger	Williams	MK	8/8/2002	$70,000.00
Annie	Philips	SH	9/12/2002	$31,000.00
Melissa	James	AC	3/1/2002	$53,500.00
Mary	Smith	AD	6/15/1989	$95,000.00

Exhibit 3-6: The tblEmployee table with two columns selected for sorting

Do it!

C-2: Sorting records by multiple fields

Here's how	Here's why
1 Click the field heading Dept	To select this column.
2 Press and hold SHIFT	
Select the Hire Date column	Click the field heading. Both fields are selected.
Release the Shift key	
3 Click 	(The Ascending button is in the Sort & Filter group.) The records are sorted in ascending order, based first on Dept and then on Hire Date, because Dept is the left-most sorted column. Small arrows appear in both field headings.
4 Click 	(The Clear All Sorts button is in the Sort & Filter group.) To clear the sorts.
5 Sort on First Name	Select the column and Ascending. You'll sort by first and last name.
6 Sort on Last Name	Records are now sorted first by Last Name because that's the last field you sorted on.
7 Clear the sorts	Click Clear All Sorts.

Filtering records by using Filter By Selection

Explanation

In Datasheet view, you can use the Filter By Selection feature to display records based on a field value. For example, if you want to view the records of the Shipping department, you can apply a filter so that only records from the SH department appear in the table, as shown in Exhibit 3-7.

To filter records by using Filter By Selection, right-click the data value you want to filter and choose the appropriate option. You can also select the value and use the filter buttons in the Sort & Filter group. You can select a whole value or just part. For instance, if you select only the first letter of the last name "Jones," and then right-click the selection, you'll have the shortcut option filter for names beginning with "J."

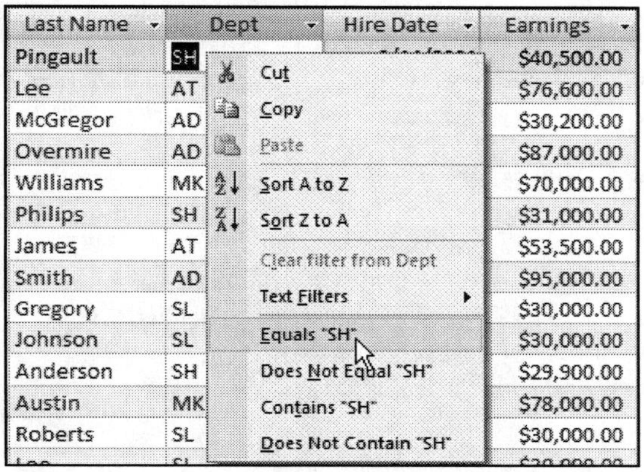

Exhibit 3-7: Filtering records from the shortcut menu.

To remove a filter, click Toggle Filter in the Sort & Filter group, or right-click within the column and select Clear filters from the shortcut menu.

Do it!

C-3: Using Filter By Selection

Here's how	Here's why
1 In the Dept column, select the value **SH** in the first record.	You'll filter records for this value.
2 In the Sort & Filter group, click 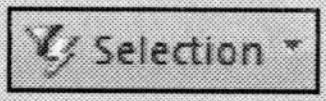	The Selection button.
Observe the options	There are several for filtering with this value.
Click the button again	To close the menu without choosing an option.
3 In the Dept Column, right-click the value **SH**.	To open the shortcut menu. It has the same filter options as above.
Choose **Equals "SH"**	(As shown in Exhibit 3-7.) To filter out all records but those where Dept is equal to SH.
Observe the Dept field heading	It has a small filter symbol, indicating a filter is active on that field.
4 Click **Toggle Filter**	(In the Sort & Filter group.) To remove the filter. The filter symbol no longer appears in the field heading.
5 In the Hire Date column, in the first record, select **2001**, as shown.	 Don't select the rest of the date. You'll filter to show only 2001 hires.
6 Right-click the selected text and choose **Ends With 2001**	The list is filtered by that year.
7 Right-click in the Hire Date column and choose **Clear filter from Hire Date**.	(Right-click in the column but not on the heading.) This removes the filter from just the selected column, while the Remove Filter button removes all filters.
8 Close the table	Do not save changes.

Filtering records by using Filter By Form

Explanation

The Filter By Form feature filters records based on a specific condition. When you use the Filter By Form feature in a table in Datasheet view, a table with empty fields appears. You can enter values in these empty fields to specify the filtering criteria.

To filter records by using Filter By Form:

1. In the Sort & Filter group, click Advanced to display a list.
2. Select Filter By Form. A blank form appears.
3. Enter criteria in the empty fields.

Do it!

C-4: Using Filter By Form

Here's how	Here's why
1 Open tblEmployee	
2 In the Sort & Filter group, click **Advanced** and select **Filter By Form**	(On the Home tab.) A filter form opens.
3 In the first row, under Earnings, enter **>50000**, as shown	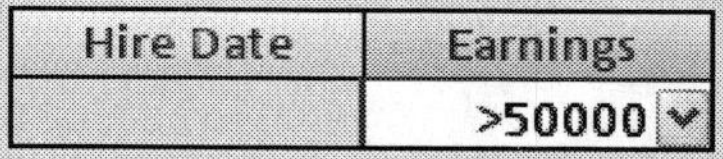 You'll display the records of employees whose earnings are greater than $50,000.
4 Click **Toggle Filter**	(In the Sort & Filter group.) The table now displays only the records of employees whose earnings are greater than $50,000.
5 Remove the filter	Click Toggle Filter.

Filtering records by using Filter Excluding Selection

Explanation

You use the Filter Excluding Selection feature to filter out (exclude) records containing a specific value. For example, you can use this feature to display the records of all employees except for those in the Accounting department.

To filter records by using Filter Excluding Selection, right-click a value you want to filter out and choose Does not Equal <*value*> or Does not Contain <*value*>.

Do it!

C-5: Using Filter Excluding Selection

Here's how	Here's why
1 In the Dept column, right-click any value **SL** and choose **Does Not Equal "SL"**	You'll filter out all the people in the sales department.
2 Remove the filter	
3 Close the table	Do not save changes.

Filtering records by using Advanced Filter/Sort

Explanation

When you use the Advanced Filter/Sort feature, you specify the criteria to filter records in a design grid. This feature helps you search for records that satisfy any specific or multiple criteria.

To filter records by using Advanced Filter/Sort, click Advanced in the Sort & Filter group, and select Advanced Filter/Sort to open the design grid. Then, specify the criteria for filtering the records.

The design grid displays the selected table in the upper pane. In the lower pane it displays columns in which you enter fields, and rows in which you specify sort and filter criteria, as shown in Exhibit 3-8.

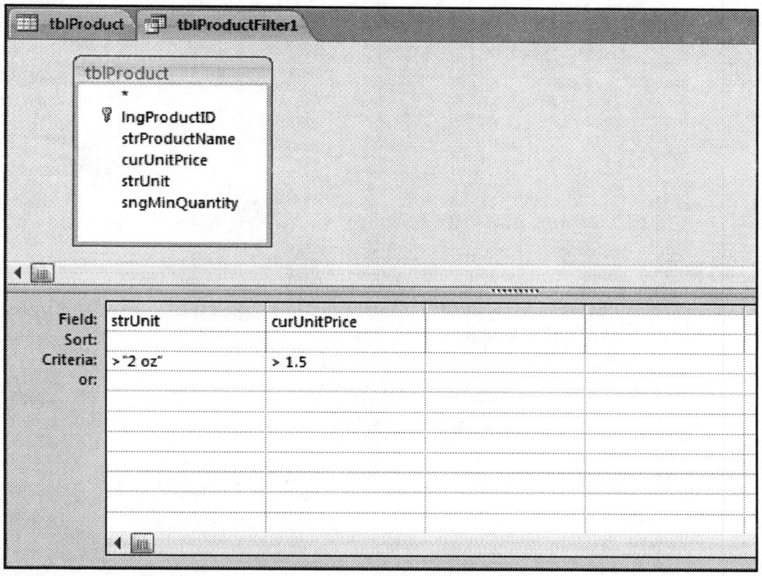

Exhibit 3-8: The design grid for an advanced filter/sort

Do it!

C-6: Using Advanced Filter/Sort

Here's how	Here's why
1 Open tblProduct	
2 Click **Advanced** and select **Advanced Filter/Sort...**	(In the Sort & Filter group.) To open the design grid. The tblProduct table appears in the upper pane. The insertion point is in the first column of the field row in the lower pane.
3 In the Field row, select **strUnit** from the list as shown	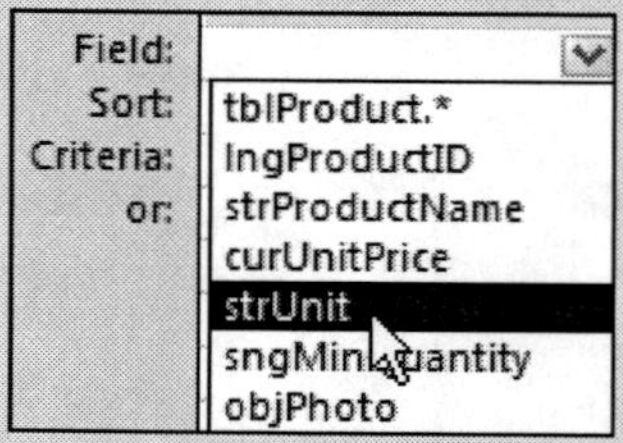 To add the strUnit field to the design grid.
Place the insertion point in the second column of the Field row	You'll add a field to the second column of the Field row.
From the list, select **curUnitPrice**	To add this field to the design grid.
4 Place the insertion point in the first column of the Criteria row	You'll specify a criterion for the field strUnit.
Enter **> 2 oz**	To view the details of products whose unit value is greater than 2 oz.
5 Place the insertion point in the second column of the criteria row	To specify a criterion for the field curUnitPrice.
Enter **> 1.5**	To view the details of products whose unit price is greater than $1.50.
6 Apply the filter	Click the Toggle Filter button. The table displays the records of the products whose current unit price is greater than $1.50 and whose unit value is greater than 2 oz.
7 Remove the filter	
8 Close the table	Do not save changes.

Deleting records

Explanation

To delete a record, select that record. Then click Delete in the Records group, press the Delete key, or right-click and select Delete Record. After a record is deleted, it cannot be restored.

Do it!

C-7: Deleting a record

Here's how	Here's why
1 Open tblProduct	You'll delete a record in this table.
2 Click as shown	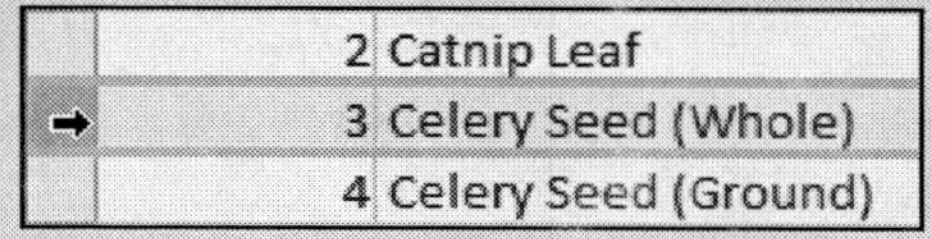 The third record contains the details for Celery Seed (Whole). A thick border now surrounds the record.
3 Click Delete	(In the Records group.) A message box appears prompting you to confirm the deletion.
4 Click **Yes**	The record in the table is deleted.
5 Press CTRL + Z	It has no effect. You cannot undo the deletion of a record.
6 Update and close the table	
7 Close the database	

Unit summary: Fields and records

Topic A In this topic, you learned how to **modify the table design** by changing the name of a **field**, and by **deleting**, **inserting**, and **moving** fields. Then, you learned how to **attach** a file to a record in a table. Finally, you learned how to create a **totals row** for a table.

Topic B In this topic, you learned how to use the **Find and Replace** dialog box to find and replace values in a table. You learned how to **undo** changes made in a record.

Topic C In this topic, you learned how to **sort** records based on single or multiple fields. You learned how to sort records in the ascending or descending order of any field. You also learned how to view selected records by applying a **filter**. You filtered records by using various methods, such as Filter By Selection, Filter By Form, Filter Excluding Selection, and Advanced Filter/Sort. Finally, you **deleted** a record.

Review questions

1 Which view is used to change the name of a field?

A Design view

B Layout view

C Field view

D Datasheet view

2 What is the first step before inserting or deleting a field?

3 By default, where are new rows inserted?

4 When deleting a field, in which of the following instance are you *not* prompted to confirm the deletion?

A The field contains data.

B The field is the primary key.

C The table has not been saved since the field was added.

D The field is a memo field.

5 What is the procedure to change a field name?

6 Which feature enables you to quickly locate records that meet specific criteria?

A The Replace feature

B The scrollbar

C The Undo feature

D The Find feature

7 What is the difference between sorting and filtering?

8 Name some of the ways to filter records.

9 When sorting records by multiple fields, which sort field takes precedence in the sort?

10 Deleted records can be restored. True or false?

Independent practice activity

In this activity, you'll compare the design of two tables, and modify one to match the other. Then, you'll check the spelling in table. Next, you'll sort and filter records.

1 Open ModifyingDatabase. Then, open the table tblNewRetailer in Design view and observe its design.

2 Open the table tblRetailer in Design view and observe its design. Compare it to the design of tblNewRetailer.

3 Modify the design of the tblRetailer table so that it matches the tblNewRetailer table, as shown in Exhibit 3-9. Save the design changes. (*Hint*: First, edit the field names to match. Then, change the data types to match. Next, drag the fields so that their order matches. Insert a strFax field. Finally, add Descriptions.)

4 Save and close the tblRetailer table.

5 Switch to Datasheet view, and sort the records by First Name in ascending order.

6 Filter records to show only records with Region field equal to NY.

7 Remove the filter.

8 Use Filter By Form to show only records with City value of Portland.

9 Save and close the tblNewRetailer table.

10 Open the tblProduct table.

11 Use Advanced Filter/Sort to find products whose unit price is greater than $5.00.

12 Save and close the table and the database.

	Field Name	Data Type	Description
🔑	lngRetailerID	AutoNumber	Unique ID automatically assigned to each Retailer
	strRetailerName	Text	Full name of Retailer
	strAddr1	Text	Address Line 1 of Retailer
	strAddr2	Text	Address Line 2 of Retailer
	strCity	Text	Retailer's City
	strRegion	Text	Retailer's State or Province (use std mailing abbreviation)
	strPostalCode	Text	Retailer's Zip or Postal Code (use Zip+4 if possible)
	strFirstName	Text	First name of purchasing agent at the Retailer
	strLastName	Text	Last name of purchasing agent at the Retailer
	strPhone	Text	Retailer's Voice Phone and extension
	strFax	Text	Retailer's Fax number
	lngRep	Number	Company Account Representative ID for this Retailer

Exhibit 3-9: The tblNewRetailer table design

Unit 4

Data entry rules

Complete this unit, and you'll know how to:

A Set properties for a field.

B Create input masks for fields, and use the Input Mask Wizard.

C Set validation rules for entering data in a field.

Topic A: Setting field properties

This topic covers the following Microsoft Certified Application Specialist exam objective for Access 2007.

#	Objective
2.4.2	**Modify field properties** • Define text length • Allow zero length • Set memo fields as append only • Set data validation rules • Enter captions • Fill a series without formatting

Field properties

Explanation

You can set properties for the fields in a table to control how data is stored and displayed in that table. For example, you can ensure that the Product ID field is never left blank or that data in the Postal Code field contains only five digits. Field properties are set in the Field Properties pane in Design view.

You can set several properties for fields in a table. The following table describes some of these properties:

Property	Description
Required	Specifies a field that cannot contain null values.
Allow Zero Length	Specifies that the field can contain null values.
Field Size	Specifies the maximum number of characters that can be entered in the field.
Append Only	For a memo field, specifies that the field can only be added to—existing data cannot be overwritten.

The Required property

The *Required* property ensures that a field does not contain a null value. (A *null value* is a value that indicates missing or unknown data in a field.) If the Required property is set to Yes, you must enter a value in the field. To set this property for a field:

1. Open the table in Design view.
2. Display the general properties of the field that you want.
3. From the Required list, select Yes.
4. Update the table. A message box appears stating that you can test the existing data for the new rule that you have set.
5. Click No to skip testing the new rule on the existing data, or click Yes to test the new rule on the existing data.

Do it!

A-1: Setting the Required property

Here's how	Here's why
1 Open DataEntryRules	From the current unit folder.
2 Open tblRetailer	
3 Click	(The Last record button is at the bottom of the tblRetailer window.) To move to the last record.
Under the Retailer Name column, enter **Magic Spices**	To specify the Retailer Name.
4 Click	(The New (blank) record button is at the bottom of the tblRetailer window.) To add another record to this table. Notice that you have not entered data in any other fields in the record.
5 Switch to Design view	
6 Place the insertion point in the **strAddr1** field, as shown	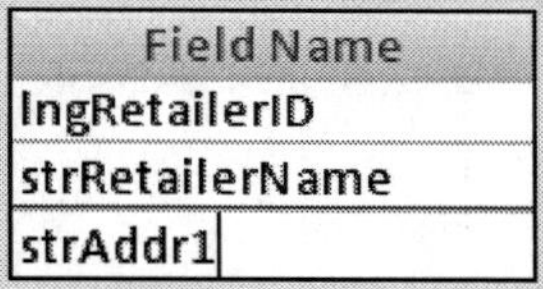 You'll set the Required property for the strAddr1 field. The general properties for the field strAddr1 appear in the General tab of the Field Properties pane.
7 From the Required list, select **Yes**, as shown	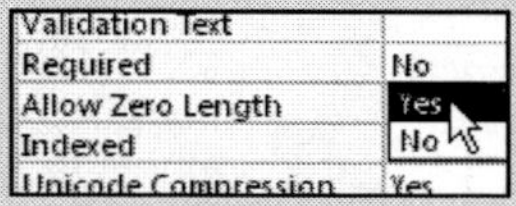 (In the Field Properties pane, General tab.) To set the Required field property.
8 Update the table	A message appears asking if you want the existing data to be tested with the new rules.
Click **No**	To skip testing the existing data for the new validation rule.
9 Switch to Datasheet view	You'll test the Required field property.

10 Add a new record	Click the New (blank) record button at the bottom of the tblRetailer window.
In the new record, under Retailer Name, enter **Spice Outlet**	
Click [New record button]	(To add another new record.) A message box appears warning that you must enter a value in the strAddr1 field. This is because the Required property has been set for this field.
Click **OK**	(To close the message box.) You'll enter a value in the Address1 field.
11 Press TAB	(If necessary.) To move to the Address1 cell.
Enter **202 Brown St**	
12 Add a new record	The message box doesn't appear.
13 Delete the records for Magic Spices and Spice Outlet	
14 Update the table	

The Allow Zero Length property

Explanation

You can set the *Allow Zero Length* property to Yes for a text, memo, or hyperlink field to make these fields accept strings of zero length, which is sometimes necessary when importing data from other sources. You can set the Allow Zero Length property to No and the Required property to Yes to ensure that the field can not contain an empty string, a null, nor a space character, all of which would make the field appear blank. For example, if you set the Required property of an E-mail field to Yes, then data must be entered in that field. If you set the Allow Zero Length property to Yes, the field can contain values with no characters. You can then enter a null value (such as a space) in the E-mail field for those individuals who do not have an e-mail account.

To set the Allow Zero Length property for a field, display the General properties for the field. From the Allow Zero Length list, select Yes.

Do it!

A-2: Using the Allow Zero Length property

Here's how	Here's why
1 Switch to Design view	
Display the General properties for the strPhone field	(Under Field Name, place the insertion point in the field strPhone.) You'll set the Required and Allow Zero Length properties of this field.
From the Required list, select **Yes**	To set the Required property.
From the Allow Zero Length list, select **Yes**	To set the Allow Zero Length property.
2 Update the table	A message box appears, stating that Access can test all the data in the table against the new rules.
Click **Yes**	To test the existing data and to save the table design.
3 Switch to Datasheet view	
4 Add a new record	
Under Retailer Name, enter **Magic Spices**	To specify the Retailer Name for the new record.
Under Address1, enter **111 SE Carnegie St**	
5 Under City, enter **Astoria**	
Under Region, enter **OR**	
Under Postal Code, enter **97102**	
6 Add a new record	A message appears stating that you must enter a value in the strPhone field.
7 Click **OK**	To close the message box.
8 Place the insertion point in the Phone field	You'll enter a null value in this column.
Press SPACEBAR	To specify a null value in the Phone column.
Add a new record	The warning message doesn't appear, which means that you can now enter null values in the Phone column. This ensures that you left the field blank on purpose.
9 Update the table	

The Field Size property

Explanation

You use the *Field Size* property to specify the maximum number of characters that can be entered in a field.

To set the Field Size property, display the general properties for the field you want. In the Field Size box, enter the field size.

Do it!

A-3: Setting the Field Size property

Here's how	Here's why
1 Switch to Design view	
Display the General properties for the field strPostalCode	
2 Edit the Field Size box to read **10**	To set the Field Size property for the field.
3 Update the table	A message box appears stating that data might be lost because of the change in the Field Size property.
Click **Yes**	To save the table so that the current values of this field do not exceed five characters.
4 Switch to Datasheet view	
Navigate to the last record	(Click the last record button at the bottom of the tblRetailer window.) You'll enter a postal code in this record.
5 In the Postal Code field in the last record, select the value as shown	TX 73344 OR 97102
Edit the field to read **97102-1234**	To enter a postal code in the U.S. Postal Service's Zip + 4 format.
Edit the field to read **97102-12345**	Access will not allow you to type the last (11th) character, because you set the Field Size property to 10.
6 Update the table	

The Append Only property

Explanation

You use the *Append Only* property for memo fields. When this property is enabled, Access keeps a history of all changes made to the field. You can view this history to see the date and time changes were made, as well as the change itself.

To set the Append Only property, display the General properties for the memo field. Scroll down to the bottom of the list. From the Append Only list, select Yes.

To view the History, select any record in the changed column. Then right-click the changed field and choose Show Column History. A dialog box displays the changes, as shown in Exhibit 4-1.

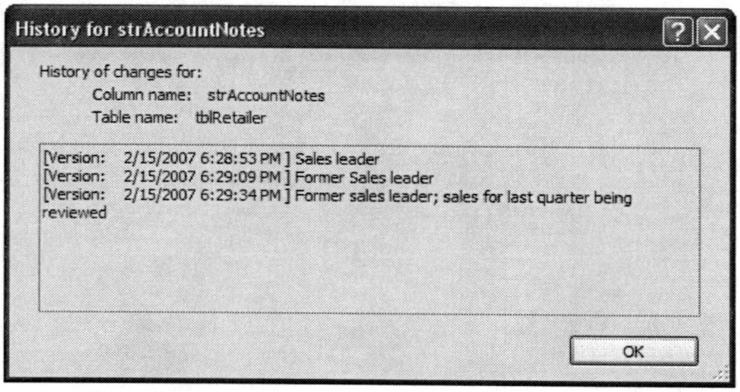

Exhibit 4-1: The History dialog box

Note that the History dialog box shows only changes to the original entry—it does not record the original entry as a change itself.

If you later disable the Append Only property, all recorded history changes are deleted.

Do it!

A-4: Setting the Append Only property

Here's how	Here's why
1 Switch to Design view	
2 Display the General properties for the field strAccountNotes	
From the Append Only list, select **Yes**	To set the Append Only property.
3 Update the table	
Switch to Datasheet view	
4 Scroll to the right	To see the Account notes field.
In the first record, type **Sales leader**	
Press TAB	Moving out of the field saves the change to the data value in the database.

5	Edit the record to read **Former sales leader**	To change the memo field for this record.
	Press TAB	To save the data value.
6	Edit the record to read **Former sales leader; sales for last quarter being reviewed**	
	Press TAB	
7	Select any record in the Account notes column	To activate the History feature.
8	Right-click the field you changed and choose **Show column history...**	The History for strAccountNotes dialog box displays.
	Observe the history changes	The date and time of the changes, as well as the changed text, display. The original entry of Sales leader is not recorded as a change.
	Click **OK**	To close the dialog box.
9	Switch to Design view	
	For the strAccountNotes field, set Append Only to **No**	
	Update the table	To save the changes to the design.
10	Switch to Datasheet view	
	In the Account notes column, right-click the changed record	The shortcut menu no longer includes Show Column History.

Topic B: Working with input masks

This topic covers the following Microsoft Certified Application Specialist exam objective for Access 2007.

#	Objective
2.4.2	**Modify field properties** • Define input masks for fields

Input masks

Explanation

An *input mask* defines how data should be entered in a field. It determines the type of data and the number of characters in it. For example, if you want all phone numbers in a table to contain only numbers and to appear in the same format, you can use an input mask such as (999) 999-9999.

The Format property defines the display format for a field or control. For example, you can format all dates in the month/day/year format or some other format. You can choose from a list of predefined formats for fields for the AutoNumber, Number, Currency, Date/Time, and Yes/No data types, or you can create your own custom format for any data type except OLE Object. The *OLE Object* data type is used to link to objects created in other applications, such as Microsoft Word.

Creating input masks

An input mask consists of literals, such as hyphens, underscores, or dashes, which separate blanks. Blanks are used as placeholders for data, and are visible only in Datasheet view. The *Input Mask* property defines a field's input mask. For example, for the phone number input mask, you enter digits into the blanks.

An input mask definition contains three sections separated by semicolons:

- The first section contains the input mask. For example, the mask 000-000-0000 specifies that the field should contain 10 numbers separated by hyphens.
- The second section determines whether to store the literal characters that are entered in the field along with the characters that have been entered in the blanks. To define a literal character, enter any character other than the valid input-mask characters, including spaces and symbols. To define one of the valid input-mask characters as a literal character, precede that character with a backslash (\). If you specify 0 in the second section of the input mask, this stores both the literal characters and the values. If you specify 1 or leave this section blank, only the values are stored. For example, for telephone number 555-333-4444, entering 0 in the second section stores 555-333-4444 in the field. Entering 1 in the second section stores 5553334444.
- The third section defines the characters that appear as placeholders for the blanks in the input mask. For example, if you specify * as a placeholder for the input mask 000-000-0000, then ***-***-**** appears in the field in the table's Datasheet view.

To create an input mask for a field:

1. Open the table in Design view.
2. Display the General properties.
3. Click the Input Mask box.
4. Enter the input mask.
5. Update the table.

Input-mask characters

Access provides several input-mask characters and has specific interpretations for each. A literal character must be preceded with a backslash (\). The following table lists some literal characters:

Character	Description
0	The user must enter a number between 0 and 9.
9	The user can enter a number or a space, but entry is optional.
#	The user can enter a number or a space. Entry is optional, and all blank positions will be converted to spaces.
L	The user must enter a letter, A through Z.
?	The user can enter a letter, but entry is optional.
A	The user must enter either a letter or a number.
a	The user can enter a letter or a number, but entry is optional.
&	The user must enter any character or a space.
C	The user can enter a character or a space, but entry is optional.
<	Any letter that follows will be converted to lowercase.
>	Any letter that follows will be converted to uppercase.
Password	Setting the Input Mask property to the word Password creates a password entry text box. Any character typed in the text box is stored as the character but is displayed as an asterisk (*).

Do it!

B-1: Creating an input mask

Here's how	Here's why
1 Switch to Design view	In tblRetailer.
2 Display the General properties for the strPhone field	
3 In the Input Mask box, enter **(999) 000-0000;0;#**	To set the Input Mask property. In the first section, the first three blanks contain 9, indicating it is not mandatory to enter values. The second section contains 0, so the literal characters will be stored with the values. The (#) character in the third section is the placeholder for the blanks.
4 Update the table	If a smart tag appears for Property Update Options, ignore it.
5 Switch to Datasheet view	You'll test the input mask by entering sample data in the table.
6 In the last record, select the Phone field.	
Observe the cell	 The (#) characters appear in the cell.
7 Select the first character and enter **ABC**	Nothing appears in the cell because the characters in the cell should always be numbers.
Enter **5033051478**	Notice that the (#) characters are replaced with the numbers you enter.
8 Update the table	

The Input Mask Wizard

Explanation

You can use the Input Mask Wizard to create an input mask based on the built-in input masks in Access. To do so:

1. Open the table in Design view.
2. Display the general properties of the field that you want to set an input mask for.
3. Click the Input Mask box, and click the Build button to display the Input Mask Wizard.
4. From the Input Mask list, select the input mask you want. Click Next.
5. In the Input Mask box, change the input mask, if necessary.
6. From the Placeholder list, select a placeholder, if necessary.
7. Select the relevant option to specify whether you want to store the literal characters with the values entered in the blanks. Click Next.
8. Click Finish to create the input mask.

Do it!

B-2: Working with the Input Mask Wizard

Here's how	Here's why
1 In the Fax field, enter **5553334444**	This field does not contain an input mask.
2 Switch to Design view	
3 Display the General properties for the strFax field	You'll set an input mask for this field.
Click the Input Mask box	The Build button appears.
Click [...]	(The Build button is next to the Input Mask box.) To display the Input Mask Wizard.
4 In the list, verify that Phone Number is selected	
Click **Next**	To move to the next step of the Input Mask Wizard.
5 In the Try It box, enter **5553334444**	The number you entered appears in the input-mask format.
Click **Next**	To move to the next step of the Input Mask Wizard.
6 Select the first option, as shown	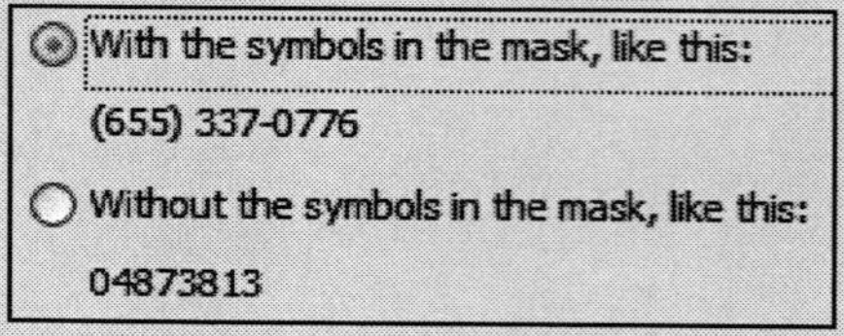 You'll store both the literal characters and the values entered in the field.
Click **Next**	To move to the next step of the Input Mask Wizard.
7 Click **Finish**	To close the Input Mask Wizard dialog box and to set the input mask for the field.
Observe the Input Mask box	 The exclamation mark in the input mask causes it to appear right to left in Datasheet view. The first three blanks in the first section contain 9, so entering these values is optional. The second section contains 0, so literals are stored with the values. The underscore in the last section (_) is the placeholder for the blanks.
8 Update the table	

9	Switch to Datasheet view	To view the data in the input-mask format. Notice that the data in the Fax column now appears in the input-mask format.
	Close the table	

Topic C: Setting validation rules

This topic covers the following Microsoft Certified Application Specialist exam objective for Access 2007.

#	Objective
2.4.2	**Modify field properties** • Set data validation rules

Validation Rules

Explanation

You use a *validation rule* to check data that has been entered into a field. As with an input mask, you can set a format template that the data must match, but with a validation rule, you can also use logical operators to check the data against multiple criteria. For instance, you can set a field to be in date format, and set it to reject dates earlier than the current day. If data entered in a field violates the validation rule, an error message appears and prompts for the correct value. You can set the text of the error message in the Validation Text property. Following are some sample validation rules:

Rule	Description
Like "S???"	The value in the field must have four characters, and the first must always be S.
<>0	The value in the field must not be equal to zero (0).
0 or >100	The value in the field must be 0 or greater than 100.
<#1/1/2007	The date in the field must be earlier than January 1, 2007.

To create a validation rule, display the General properties of the field for which you want to set it, then in the Validation Rule box, enter the validation rule.

Do it!

C-1: Creating validation rules

Here's how	Here's why
1 Open tblProduct in Design view	
Display the General properties for the strUnit field	You'll set a validation rule for this field.
2 In the Validation Rule box, enter **Like "* oz" Or Like "* lb"**	(To set the Validation Rule property.) In the validation rule, "Like" is used to specify that the strUnit field should be entered in the format of the characters you specify after the word Like. The validation rule specifies that the values you enter in the field should end with either "oz" or "lb."
3 Update the table	A message box appears, asking if you want the existing data to be tested with the new rule.
Click **Yes**	To save the table's design and to test the existing data against the new validation rule.
4 Switch to Datasheet view	You'll try to change a value in the Unit field.
Navigate to the first record	
5 In the first record edit the value in the Unit field to read **50 g**	For 50 grams.
Press TAB	A message box appears, warning that the data you entered violates the field's validation rule.
Click **OK**	You'll enter the correct unit in this cell.
6 Change the Unit to **2 oz**	
Press TAB	No warning message appears.
7 Update the table	

The Validation Text property

Explanation

When you enter data that violates a field's validation rule, Access displays a message box. This message can be rather cryptic and hard to understand for the end user, who might not know the underlying field names. You can set the *Validation Text* property to specify the error message in this message box.

To set validation text for a field, display the General properties of the field, and in the Validation Text box, enter the text that you want to display in the message box.

Do it!

C-2: Setting validation text

Here's how	Here's why
1 Switch to Design view	You'll specify the validation text for a validation rule, so that the warning in the message box is easier to understand.
2 Display the General properties of the strUnit field	If necessary.
In the Validation Text box, enter **The values in the Unit field must end in "oz" or "lb"**	To set the Validation Text property for this field.
3 Update the table	
4 Switch to Datasheet view	You'll test the Validation Text property.
5 Navigate to the first record	You'll try to change the Unit for this record.
Change the Unit to **50 g**	
Press TAB	A message box appears, displaying the validation text that you set.
6 Click **OK**	(To close the message box.) You'll enter the correct unit.
Change the Unit to **2 oz**	
7 Close the table	
Close the database	

Unit summary: Data entry rules

Topic A

In this topic, you learned how to set the **Required**, **Allow Zero Length**, **Field Size**, and **Append Only** properties for a field. You learned that by setting these **field properties** you could control how data is displayed and stored in a table.

Topic B

In this topic, you learned how to set **input masks** for a field in a table by entering the input mask in a field's Property Sheet. You learned that an input mask specifies the format for entering data in a field. You also learned how to set the input mask by using the **Input Mask Wizard**.

Topic C

In this topic, you learned how to set a **validation rule** for a field. In addition, you learned how to set **validation text** for a field. You learned how to display customized messages by setting validation text.

Review questions

1 Which field property is used to specify that the field can contain null values?

A Allow Zero Length

B Required

C Field Size

D Format

2 Which field property is used to guarantee that the field is not left to appear blank? (Choose all that apply.)

A Required

B Allow Zero Length

C Field Size

D Format

3 What is the definition of a null value?

4 Describe the three sections of an input mask.

5 When creating an input mask, how do you indicate literal characters?

6 Identify the correct character for each of the following:

Description	Character
The user must enter a number between 0 and 9.	
The user can enter a number (0 through 9) or a space, but entry is optional.	
The users must enter a letter, A through Z.	
The user can enter a letter (A through Z), but entry is optional.	
The user can enter a number or a space. Entry is optional, and all blank positions will be converted to spaces.	

7 Which field property is used to display a customized error message?

A Default Value

B Validation Test

C Validation Text

D Field Message Text

Independent practice activity

In this activity, you will set a field's required property, create an input mask, set a field's default value, and create a validation rule.

1 Open DefiningDataEntryRules.

2 Set the Required property for the strProductName field of the tblProduct table to Yes.

3 Update and close the table.

4 Create an input mask for the strPhone field in the tblRetailer table. Edit the input mask to read **000\-000\-0000;1;***. This will ensure that only 10 numbers are entered in the field, and although the input mask will display numbers in a specific format in the table, only the numbers (not the literal characters) are stored in the table. The asterisk (*) is used as a placeholder.

5 Update the table.

6 Test the input mask by entering sample data.

7 Close the table without saving.

8 Create a validation rule for the dtmOrderDate field in the tblOrder table to ensure that the dates entered are after 1/1/2007. (*Hint*: Enter the validation rule **>#1/1/2007#** in the Validation Rule box.) Do not apply the rule to existing data. Set validation text for the rule.

9 Update the table.

10 Test the validation rule by entering sample data.

11 Close the table without saving.

12 Close the database.

Unit 5
Basic queries

Complete this unit, and you'll know how to:

A Plan, create, save, and run queries; and use queries to sort data and to filter query results.

B Modify queries and query results by adding fields, and find records with empty fields.

C Perform operations in queries by using comparison operators; use AND and OR conditions in queries; and use expressions and aggregate functions.

Topic A: Creating and using queries

This topic covers the following Microsoft Certified Application Specialist exam objectives for Access 2007.

#	Objective
4.1.1	**Create queries based on single tables** • Add fields to queries • Add all fields from a table to a query
4.1.6	**Save filters as queries**
4.2.1	**Add tables to and remove tables from queries** • Add tables to queries
4.2.2	**Add criteria to queries** • Hard-coded criteria
5.1.2	**Sort data within queries**
5.2.2	**Filter data within queries**

Using queries to retrieve data

Explanation

A *query* is a database object that retrieves and displays selective data from one or more tables or from other queries. You can use a query to retrieve data meeting specific conditions. For example, if you want to see all the products with a unit price greater than $2, you can specify this condition in a query.

The results of a query display in Datasheet view. The result fields in a query datasheet use the formats and properties set in the base table. You can edit, navigate, sort, and filter these results just as you would do in a table in Datasheet view. A *filter* is a set of conditions applied to data to view a section of data. Query results are similar to the results of a filter, but a query is a database object that you can save permanently, whereas a filter provides only a temporary view.

To extract data by using a query, you need to plan and define the following:

- The conditions that you want the data to meet
- The fields that you want to see in the query result
- The tables from which you'll extract the fields
- The statements that you'll use to extract data

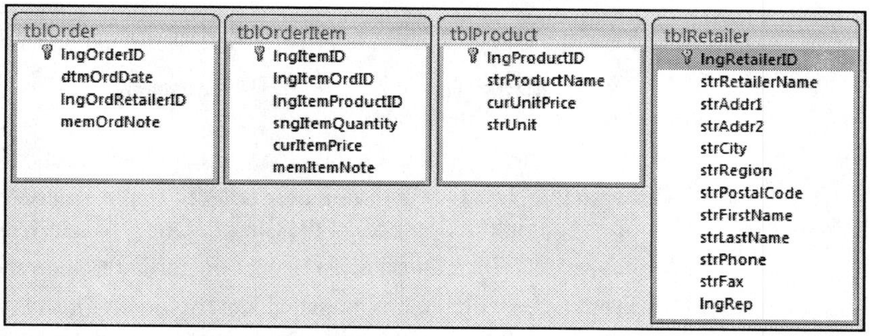

Exhibit 5-1: The tables in a database

Do it!

A-1: Planning a query

Questions and answers

1 You have designed a database containing the tables shown in Exhibit 5-1. With respect to these tables, answer the following:

You need to extract product details for all records with a unit price greater than $3. On what field would the condition apply?

You want to display the details of the retailers in a specific city that is in a specific region. On what fields would this condition apply, and from which table would you extract this information?

What fields would you want to display when you run the query to display records with a unit price greater than $3?

Basic queries

Explanation

You can use the Query Wizard to retrieve data from one or more tables or queries:

1. Switch to Datasheet view (if necessary).
2. Activate the Create tab.
3. In the Other group, click the arrow under Query and choose Query Wizard.
4. From the New Query dialog box, select Simple Query Wizard and click OK to open the first dialog box of the Simple Query Wizard, as shown in Exhibit 5-2.
5. From the Tables/Queries list, select the table that you want to base the query on.
6. From the Available Fields list, select the fields for the query, and add them to the Selected Fields list. Click Next to move to the next dialog box.
7. Select the relevant option to display either detailed results or a summary of the query result. This dialog box will appear only if you select a numeric field for your query. Click Next. In the What title do you want for your query? box, specify a title for the query.
8. Select the option to either open the query or modify its design. Click Finish to exit the wizard and create the query.

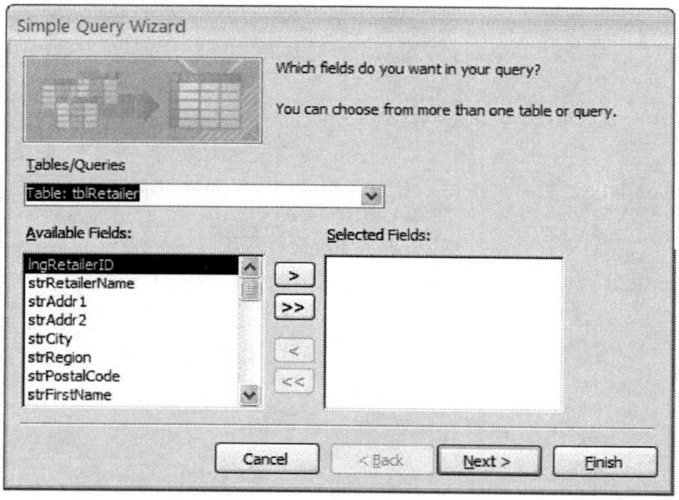

Exhibit 5-2: The Query Wizard

Do it!

A-2: Using the Query Wizard

Here's how	Here's why
1 Open the database CreateQuery	(From the current unit folder.) You'll create a query to view the names and addresses of the retailers from the tblRetailer table.
2 Activate the Create tab	
3 In the Other group, click **Query Wizard**	 To launch the New Query dialog box.
4 From the dialog box, select **Simple Query Wizard**	(If necessary.) You'll create a query by using the wizard.
Click **OK**	To open the Simple Query Wizard.
5 From the Tables/Queries list, select **Table: tblRetailer**	(You'll create the query based on this table.) The fields of the selected table, tblRetailer, appear in the Available Fields list, as shown in Exhibit 5-2.
6 Click [>>]	To add all of the fields from tblRetailer to the query. The entire contents of the Available Fields list moves to the Selected Fields list. You'll change this to use only selected fields from the table.
Click [<<]	To move all of the fields back to the Available Fields list.
7 From the Available Fields list, select **strRetailerName**	
Click [>]	(The Add button is on the Simple Query Wizard.) To add the field to the Selected Fields list.
Add **strAddr1** to the Selected Fields list	Select the field from the Available Fields list, and click the Add button.
Click **Next**	To move to the next step of the wizard.

8	Edit the What title do you want for your query? box to read **qryRetailerDetails**	This will be the title of the query.
	Verify that the first option is selected, as shown	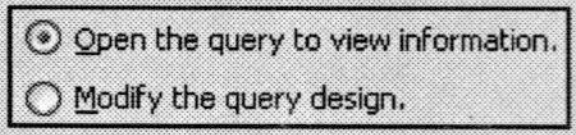 You'll view the query results as soon as you finish creating the query.
9	Click **Finish**	To view the query results in Datasheet view. The retailers' names and addresses appear in the query result. By default, the record selector is on the first record.
10	Close the query	
11	From the Navigation Pane heading list, select **All Access Objects**	(If necessary.) To display the new query in the Navigation Pane. You can double-click it any time you want to see it. A query refers to its source tables every time it is run and will reflect the latest changes in the tables.

Creating queries in Design view

Explanation

You can use Design view to create or modify queries. For basic queries, Design view contains a design grid in its lower pane, as shown in Exhibit 5-3. In its upper pane, Design view contains the field list for the table or tables on which the query is based. A field list displays all the fields in the record source. To create a query, you must select one or more data sources and define the specifications of the query in Design view. The source for the queries can be other queries or tables.

To create a basic query in Design view:

1. Open the database.
2. On the Create tab, click Query Design.
3. In the Show Table dialog box, select the table you want to add to the query, and click Add. Then click Close to return to Design view.
4. Select the fields that you want to display in the query result. Apply any sorts or criteria to the fields.
5. Click the Run button or switch to Datasheet view to see the results.

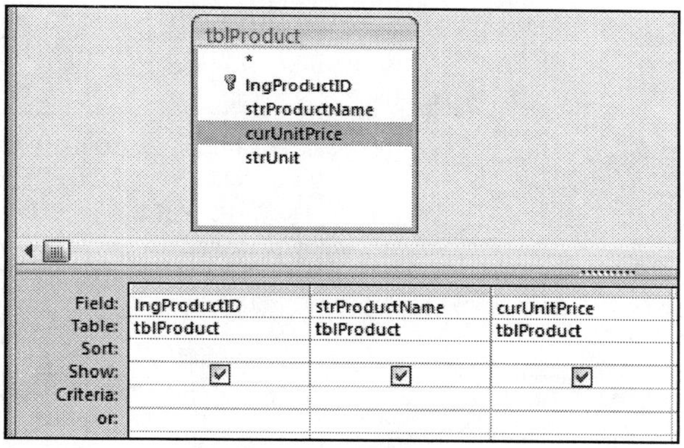

Exhibit 5-3: Creating a query in Design view

Do it!

A-3: Creating a query in Design view

Here's how	Here's why
1 On the Create tab, click the Query Design button	To open a new query in Design view, and display the Show Table dialog box.
2 Verify that the Tables tab is activated	In the dialog box.
3 Select **tblProduct**	The query will be based on this table.
Click **Add**	To add the table to the upper pane in Design view.
Click **Close**	To close the Show Table dialog box.
4 Observe Design view	The upper pane displays the field list for the tblProduct table.

5	In the lower pane of the design grid, verify that the insertion point is in the first cell of the Field row	You'll enter a field here.
6	Display the field list in the first cell of the Field row	 The field list contains the table name with an asterisk (*) and the names of all the fields in the table.
7	From the list, select **tblProduct.***	To add all fields in the table to the query.
	Observe the design grid.	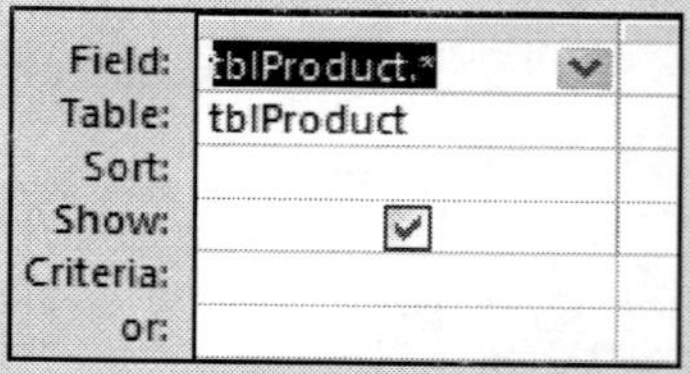 Adding the table name with its asterisk adds all fields in that table. You'll change this to use only selected table fields in the query.
8	From the list, select **lngProductID**	To add this field to the design grid.
	Observe the design grid	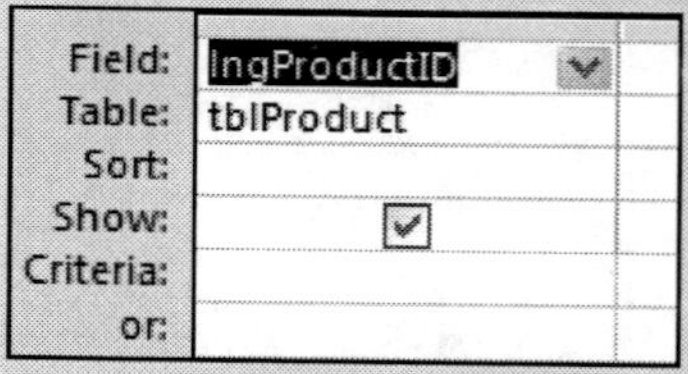 The design grid displays lngProductID in the first cell of the Field row. tblProduct appears in the Table row, and the check box in the Show row is checked. This indicates that the field lngProductID will appear in the query result.
9	In the upper pane, in the table field list, double-click **strProductName**	This is another way to add fields to the query.
10	Add **curUnitPrice** to the design grid	Double-click it in the upper pane or select it from the third field list in the lower pane.
	Observe the design grid	The design grid displays the fields lngProductID, strProductName, and curUnitPrice, as shown in Exhibit 5-3. These three fields will appear in the query result.

Saving and viewing query results

Explanation

You can save a query by clicking the Office Button and choosing Save, or by clicking the Save button on the Quick Access Toolbar. If you try to close an unsaved query, you'll be asked if you want to save it.

To see the results of the query, you must run it. To run the query, click Run in the Results group on the Design tab, or just switch to Datasheet view. The results of a query are shown in Exhibit 5-4.

qrySimpleQuery

Product II	Product Name	Unit Pric
1	Cassia	$3.00
2	Catnip Leaf	$2.75
3	Celery Seed (Whole)	$1.75
4	Celery Seed (Ground)	$1.50

Exhibit 5-4: Query results

Do it!

A-4: Saving and running the query

Here's how	Here's why
1 Click 	The first time you use this button to save an object, the Save As dialog box opens. After the first time, the button updates the object.
2 Edit the query name to read **qryPrices**	
Click **OK**	(To save the query with the specified name.) The tab of the Design window displays the name qryPrices and the name appears in the Navigation Pane.
3 Click **Run**	 (On the Design tab, in the Results group.) The results window appears, as shown in Exhibit 5-4. The fields Product ID, Product Name, and Unit Price appear in Datasheet view. The record selector is on the first record.

Sorting query results in Design view

Explanation

Sorting refers to organizing records either in ascending order or in descending order based on the contents of a field. You can sort query results in the same way that you sort records in a table. The sort order is evaluated from left to right. The left sort field is the primary sort field. You can save the sort order with the query object. If you do not specify any sort order, the records are sorted by the primary key field of the table.

To sort records in a query:

1. In the design grid, place the insertion point in the preferred cell of the Sort row. A drop-down arrow appears in the right corner of the cell.
2. Display the Sort list, and select a sort order.
3. Run the query.

Do it!

A-5: Sorting query results

Here's how	Here's why
1 Switch to Design view	
2 Place the insertion point in the third column of the Sort row	(Under curUnitPrice.) To sort the records based on the field curUnitPrice.
3 Display the Sort list, as shown	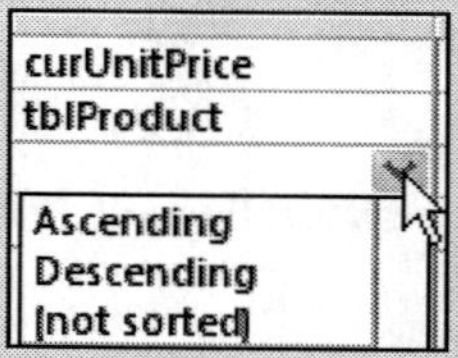
4 Select **Descending**	(To arrange the records in descending order of curUnitPrice.) In the third cell of the Sort row, Descending is selected.
5 Run the Query	Click the Run button or switch to Datasheet view.
Observe the results	The records in the query results are sorted based on the descending order of the values in the Unit Price field.

Specifying criteria to filter queries

Explanation

You can filter records by specifying criteria. You use criteria to specify a condition in the design grid to display specific records. For example, you can specify criteria to view the products sold on a specific date, or view the products whose unit price is greater than a specific value, or view the records that contain a specific value for a specific field. To add a criterion to a query, enter it in the Criteria row, and run the query.

Do it!

A-6: Filtering a query by adding criteria

Here's how	Here's why
1 Switch to Design view	You'll specify a query criterion for the field lngProductID.
2 Place the insertion point in the first cell of the Criteria row	
3 Enter **3**	This query criterion will display details about the product with Product ID 3 in the query result.
4 Run the query	
Observe the query result	It shows the Product Name and Unit Price for Product ID 3.
Update and close the query	

Creating queries from filters

Explanation

When you filter a table, you can save the filter as a query. The results of the query are the same as the results of the filter.

To create a query from a filter:

1. Filter a table according to any desired criteria.
2. Click the Office Button and choose Save As.
3. In the Save As dialog box, enter a name, and select Query from the As list. Then click OK.

Do it!

A-7: Creating a query from a filter

Here's how	Here's why
1 Open tblEmployee	From the current unit folder. You'll filter the data in this table, then create a query from that filter.
2 Place the insertion point in the first record in the **Earnings** column	
Click **Filter**	(On the Home tab.) The Filter menu appears.
3 Choose **Number Filters, Greater Than...**	The Custom Filter dialog box appears.
In the Earnings is greater than or equal to box, enter **40000**	You'll filter the employees by those that earn more than $40,000.
Click **OK**	To close the dialog box and filter the table. The number of records displayed is reduced.
4 Click the Office Button	
Choose **Save As...**	The Save As dialog box appears.
5 Edit the Save 'tblEmployee' to box to read **qryEmp40k**	The new query appears.
In the As list, select **Query**	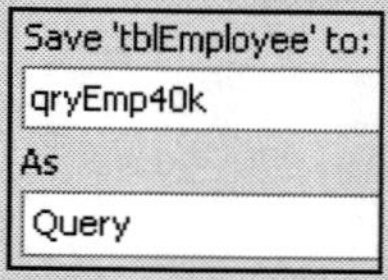 To save this as a query.
Click **OK**	The Microsoft Office Access dialog box appears, asking if you want to save the table.
6 Click **Yes**	To save the table before creating a query based on it.

7	Observe the number of records in the query	(Look to the Status bar at the bottom of the window.) There are 15 employees who earn at least $40,000.
	Close the query	
8	In tblEmployee, clear the filter	Click Toggle Filter on the Home tab.
	In record 3, edit Melinda McGregor's earnings to read **$40,200.00**	To change her salary from $30,200 to $40,200.
	Click anywhere on the table	To save the change to that record.
9	Run qryEmp40k	Double-click the query in the Navigation pane.
	Observe the number of records	This query now returns 16 records instead of 15.
	Observe the third record	Melinda McGregor is now included in the results of this query.
10	Close the table and the query	

Topic B: Modifying query results and queries

This topic covers the following Microsoft Certified Application Specialist exam objective for Access 2007.

#	Objective
4.1.1	**Create queries based on single tables** • Add fields to queries

Editing query results in Datasheet view

Explanation

Queries are not just data to look at—you can edit the results of a query, and the corresponding data changes in the query's source tables. You can modify the query itself any time by returning to Design view.

Unlike data in a static report, the data in a query are still connected to their source tables. If you change the records shown in the query result, those changes are reflected in the table on which the query is based. To edit a record in a query result, enter the new values in Datasheet view and save the query result. You can then open the source table to view the edited values.

Do it!

B-1: Editing query results

Here's how	Here's why
1 Open qryPrices	You'll edit the query results.
In the record, change Unit Price to **2.35**	(To edit a value in the query result in Datasheet view.) This will be the new value for the Unit Price of the product with the Product ID 3.
Update the query	This also updates the table on which the query is based.
2 Close the query	Save changes if prompted.
3 Open **tblProduct** in Datasheet view	(Double-click it in the Navigation Pane.) You'll check whether the value you changed in the query result is reflected in the source table.
Observe the record with the Product ID 3	The Unit Price for this product is now $2.35. The value modified in the query result is reflected in the source table.
4 Close the table	

Modifying the query design

Explanation

To edit a query, open it in Design view. You can add and remove fields, change sorting, and add criteria.

Do it!

B-2: Adding fields to a query

Here's how	Here's why
1 Open qryPrices in Design view	You'll modify your earlier query by adding the field strUnit to it.
2 Delete **3** from the Criteria row	To delete the criteria set to display only details about the product with Product ID 3.
3 Place the insertion point in the fourth cell of the Field row	You'll add another field to the query.
4 From the field list, select **strUnit**	To add this field to the query.
5 Run the query	The query result now contains one additional field, Unit.

Records with empty fields

Explanation

An empty field sometimes causes problems in a table. For example, if you want to multiply values in the fields Quantity and Price Paid, and if one of these fields does not contain a value, you'll get an incorrect result. You might want to display or remove fields that don't contain values. Unknown (empty) values in fields are referred to as *null* values. Null values cannot be entered in the primary key field, nor can they be used in calculations. You can specify Is Null in the field criteria to find all records where no entry has been made in a specific field.

To search for records that contain null values, enter Is Null in the specific cell in the Criteria row, and run the query.

Do it!

B-3: Finding records with empty fields

Here's how	Here's why
1 Switch to Design view	
2 Place the insertion point in the fourth cell of the Criteria row	(Under strUnit.) You'll search for records that do not have any values in the strUnit field.
3 Enter **Is Null**	This criterion ensures that the records with null values in the strUnit field appear in the query result.
4 Run the query	A record with an empty Unit field appears.

Topic C: Performing operations in queries

This topic covers the following Microsoft Certified Application Specialist exam objectives for Access 2007.

#	Objective
4.2.4	**Create calculated fields in queries** • Add fields to calculations • Use arithmetic operators
4.2.6	**Create sum, average, min/max, and count queries** • Create sum queries • Create average queries • Create min/max queries • Create count queries

Creating calculated fields

Explanation

You can perform comparison operations or calculations by using queries. To view records based on multiple conditions, add criteria to a query by using the comparison operators. To create a query containing multiple criteria, use the AND condition or the OR condition. You can also add a specific criterion in the query for a text field by using a wildcard operator.

You can perform calculations on existing field values. For example, you can calculate discounts for products based on values in the Unit Price field in the tblProduct table. To calculate values based on the fields in a table, you don't need to add a new field to the table to store the calculated values. Instead, you can use a query object to create a calculated field from the data in the source table. The calculated values are not stored in the source table, so they do not require more computer memory space. Calculations are performed each time the query is run, so the calculated field always contains the latest value. To perform calculations on a group of records, you can use aggregate functions, such as Sum, Avg, Count, or Min, in Design view.

Comparison operators

You use a comparison operator in a query to find records with matching values in one or more fields. A comparison operator is a symbol such as > (greater than) or < (less than). For example, you can search for all records with a unit price greater than (>) 2.35.

Comparison operators also specify a condition for a query. To use a comparison operator, place the insertion point in the proper cell of the Criteria row. Enter the criteria by using a comparison operator, and run the query.

The following table lists the comparison operators:

Operator	Description
>	Greater than
<	Less than
=	Equal to
<=	Less than or equal to
>=	Greater than or equal to
<>	Not equal to

Do it!

C-1: Using comparison operators

Here's how	Here's why
1 Switch to Design view	
2 Delete the previous criterion	(Select Is Null, and press Delete.) You'll edit this query to specify a criterion using a comparison operator.
3 Place the insertion point in the third cell of the Criteria row	
4 Enter **>2.3**	To enter a query for viewing the details of products whose Unit Price is greater than $2.30.
5 Run the query	The records with a Unit Price greater than $2.30 appear in the result.

OR conditions

Explanation

You can specify two conditions in the criteria and display the records that satisfy either condition. For example, you might want to see records whose unit price is greater than $2 or whose unit is equal to 2 oz. To display these records, you can use an OR condition for specifying the criteria.

To filter query results with the OR condition, enter the condition in the proper cell(s) of the row in the design grid, and run the query.

Do it!

C-2: Using the OR condition

Here's how	Here's why
1 Switch to Design view	
2 Delete the previous criterion	
3 Place the insertion point in the third cell of the Criteria row	(If necessary.) You will enter a criterion for the field curUnitPrice.
4 Enter **>2**	You want to find records with a Unit Price greater than $2.00.
5 Place the insertion point in the fourth cell of the **or** row	Under strUnit.
6 Enter **>1.5 oz**	This will be the criterion for strUnit.
7 Run the query	Products appear that have either a unit price greater than $2.00 or a unit greater than 1.5 oz, or both.

AND conditions

Explanation

When you use more than one condition in a query, you might want the query result to show the records that satisfy all the conditions. For example, you can search for products with a unit price greater than $1.40 and less than $1.90. Here, you can use the AND condition. The query result will show only the records that satisfy both conditions.

To use an AND condition, enter the AND condition in the proper cell of the Criteria row, and run the query.

Do it!

C-3: Using the AND condition

<table>
<tr><th>Here's how</th><th>Here's why</th></tr>
<tr><td>1 Switch to Design view</td><td></td></tr>
<tr><td>2 Delete both previous criteria</td><td></td></tr>
<tr><td>3 Place the insertion point in the third cell of the Criteria row</td><td>(If necessary.) You'll enter a criterion for curUnitPrice.</td></tr>
<tr><td>4 Enter >1.4 and <1.9</td><td></td></tr>
<tr><td>5 Run the query</td><td>
<table>
<tr><th>Product I</th><th>Unit Pric</th><th>Unit</th></tr>
<tr><td>30</td><td>$1.89</td><td>1.5 oz</td></tr>
<tr><td>28</td><td>$1.89</td><td>3 oz</td></tr>
<tr><td>4</td><td>$1.50</td><td>1 oz</td></tr>
<tr><td>27</td><td>$1.49</td><td></td></tr>
<tr><td>26</td><td>$1.49</td><td>0.5 oz</td></tr>
<tr><td>31</td><td>$1.45</td><td>2 oz</td></tr>
</table>
The results show those products that have a unit price greater than 1.40 and less than 1.90.</td></tr>
</table>

Wildcard operators

Explanation

Wildcard operators are used to retrieve multiple values. For instance, you might be looking for records that start with a certain letter or letters. You can use a wildcard operator to specify criteria. *Wildcards* are operators that you can use as placeholders.

Two frequently used wildcard operators include the question mark (?) and the asterisk (*). The question mark is used to substitute for a single character. The asterisk is used to substitute for any number of characters.

For example, if you set the criteria on a first name field to A*, a query would return all names beginning with A. If you set the criteria to A??, you would get Ann and Amy, but not Alex and Atoz, because the question marks specify a single character each. Only three-letter names that start with A would be returned.

When you use an asterisk in the criteria, Access inserts a Like operator and surrounds the character and the * with double quotation marks. A Like operator is used to search for specific text.

Do it!

C-4: Using the * wildcard

Here's how	Here's why
1 Switch to Design view	
2 Delete the previous criterion	
3 Place the insertion point in the second cell of the Criteria row	(Under strProductName.) You'll use a wildcard operator.
4 Enter **A***	To search for all products whose name starts with A.
Press TAB	To move to the next cell. The criterion under strProductName changes to Like "A*".
5 Run the query	The results show product details only for product names beginning with A.

Using calculations

Explanation

An *expression* is a combination of symbols—identifiers, operators, and values—that produces a result. An expression can include the normal arithmetic operators for addition (+), subtraction (-), multiplication (*), and division (/). When creating a calculated field, you must enclose field names referenced in an expression in square brackets.

To use calculations in a query, enter the expression in the proper cell of the Field row, and run the query.

Product I	Product Name	Unit Pric	Product Name	Discount
34	Chives (Bulk)	$17.00	Chives (Bulk)	1.7
33	Cinnamon Ground (Bulk)	$14.89	Cinnamon Ground (Bulk)	1.489
29	Carob Pods	$12.49	Carob Pods	1.249
12	De Arbol Peppers (Whole)	$5.50	De Arbol Peppers (Whole)	0.55
11	De Arbol Pepper (Ground)	$4.25	De Arbol Pepper (Ground)	0.425
7	Chinese Star Anise (Ground)	$3.50	Chinese Star Anise (Ground)	0.35
1	Cassia	$3.00	Cassia	0.3
2	Catnip Leaf	$2.75	Catnip Leaf	0.275
32	Caraway Seed	$2.50	Caraway Seed	0.25
3	Celery Seed (Whole)	$2.35	Celery Seed (Whole)	0.235
24	Cinnamon Ground	$2.29	Cinnamon Ground	0.229
6	Chili Pepper Powder	$2.00	Chili Pepper Powder	0.2
10	Cilantro Flakes	$2.00	Cilantro Flakes	0.2
25	Cinnamon (Ground) Extra High Oil	$1.99	Cinnamon (Ground) Extra High Oil	0.199
30	Carob Powder (Raw)	$1.89	Carob Powder (Raw)	0.189

Exhibit 5-5: Query results from calculations

Do it!

C-5: Using calculations in a query

Here's how	Here's why
1 Switch to Design view	
2 Delete the previous criterion	
3 Place the insertion point in the fifth cell of the Field row	To enter an expression to calculate a discount.
4 Enter the following code: `Discount:[curUnitPrice]*0.1`	To calculate the discount as 10% of the Unit Price. Here, the calculated field is Discount.
5 Run the query	(The results appear, as shown in Exhibit 5-5.) A new field, Discount, appears in the table. This field contains the calculated discount values.
6 Update and close the query	

Calculating totals

Explanation

You can perform calculations on groups of records instead of on single records. For example, while viewing a set of records containing information about products sold in each order, you can view the total sales of these same products. To calculate values for a group of records, you can use *aggregate functions* by adding the values to the Total row of the query design grid. The Total row appears in the design grid when you click the Totals button in the Show/Hide group.

You use the Sum aggregate function to total the values for a field. The Max and Min aggregate functions are used to find the maximum and minimum values of a field. You can use the Group By calculation to group records based on similar field values.

Do it!

C-6: Totaling a group of records

Here's how	Here's why
1 Open **tblOrderItem**	
Observe the table	You'll calculate the total paid for each order. Several records contain the same value for Order ID, meaning they were part of the same order. You can create a query to total the values in the field Price Paid grouped by Order ID.
2 Activate the Create tab	
3 In the Other group, click **Query Design**	 To start a new query in Design view and open the New Query dialog box. You'll use the new query to total the values in the field curItemPrice grouped by lngItemOrdID.
4 Add tblOrderItem to the query	In the Show Table dialog box, select tblOrderItem, click Add, and then click Close.
5 Add the fields lngItemOrdID and curItemPrice to the Field row	
6 Click **Totals**	 (In the Show/Hide group.) The Total row appears. In the Total row, Group By appears.
Place the insertion point in the second cell of the Total row	

7 Display the Total list

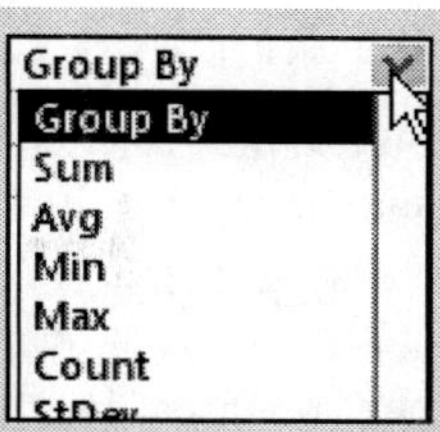

8 From the list, select **Sum**

To calculate the sum of the values in the field curItemPrice.

9 Run the query

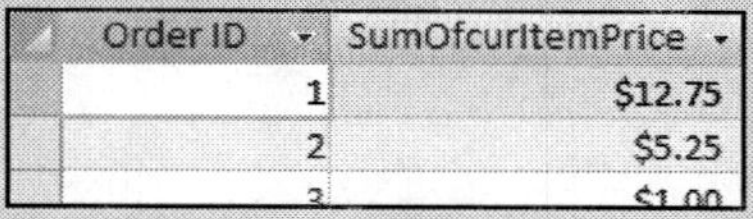

The heading Price Paid changes to SumOfcurItemPrice. Under this heading, the sum of the price paid in each order appears.

10 Save the query as **qryTotals**

11 Close the query

Close the table

The Avg and Count functions

Explanation

You use the Avg aggregate function to find the average of the values in a field for a group of records. For example, you can calculate the average sales of each product.

To find the number of values in a field, you use the Count aggregate function. For example, you can find out the number of products having the same unit price. The Count function does not count fields with null (blank) values.

Do it!

C-7: Using the Avg and Count functions

Here's how	Here's why
1 Create a new query in Design view	(On the Create tab, click Query Design.) You'll create a query to find the average sales of each product.
2 Add tblOrderItem to the query	Add the table, and close the Show Table dialog box.
3 Add the fields lngItemProductID and sngItemQuantity to the Field row	
4 Add the Totals row	Click Totals in the Show/Hide group.
5 From the Total list under the field sngItemQuantity, select **Avg**	You'll calculate the average quantity sold for each product.
6 Run the query	The average quantity sold for each product appears under the heading AvgOfsngItemQuantity.
7 Switch to Design view	
8 Place the insertion point in the first cell of the Total row	(Under lngItemProductID.) You'll now find the number of products sold in each order.
From the Total list, select **Count**	To calculate the total number of values in the field lngItemProductID.
9 Place the insertion point in the second cell of the Field row	
From the field list, select **lngItemOrdID**	You'll find the number of products sold in each order.
10 Under lngItemOrdID, from the Total list, select **Group By**	This will group the records with the same Order ID.
11 Run the query	The number of products sold for each order appears under the heading CountOflngItemProductID.
12 Save the query as **qryCalculations**	

The Min and Max functions

Explanation

The Min and Max aggregate functions return the smallest and largest values in a field.

Do it!

C-8: Using the Min and Max functions

Here's how	Here's why
1 Switch to Design view	You'll edit the query to find the maximum and minimum amount sold for each product.
2 Place the insertion point in the second cell of the Field row	
From the field list, select **sngItemQuantity**	You'll find the number of products sold in each order.
From the Total list, select **Max**	To calculate the maximum value in the field sngItemQuantity.
3 Place the insertion point in the first cell of the Total row	(Under lngItemProductID.)
From the Total list, select **Group by**	This will group the records with the same Order ID.
4 Run the query	The maximum amount of each product sold appears under the heading MaxOfsngItemQuantity.
5 Switch to Design view	You'll query for the minimum amount.
Under sngItemQuantity, from the Total list, select **Min**	
Run the query	The minimum amount of each product ordered displays. (In some cases where a product was ordered only once, the maximum amount and the minimum amount are the same.)
6 Close the query and the database	

Unit summary: Basic queries

Topic A

In this topic, you learned how to plan and create a **query**. You also created a query by using the **Query Wizard** and Design view. You saved and ran a query. You **sorted** and **filtered** records in the query datasheet.

Topic B

In this topic, you learned how to **modify values** in the query result. You changed the values in the source table by modifying the values in the query result. You also **added** and **removed** fields in query Design view. You modified a query by adding fields. You also learned how to use Is Null in the Criteria row to locate null values in a table.

Topic C

In this topic, you used **comparison operators** and separated multiple queries on a field by using the **AND** and **OR** conditions. You also used the **asterisk (*) wildcard operator** to view specific text values. You added a **calculated field** to a query by using an **expression**. You also learned how to use **aggregate functions** to perform calculations on groups of records.

Review questions

1 What is a query?

2 If both queries and filters display data based on selection criteria, how are queries and filters different?

3 When using the Query Wizard, what information do you need to provide?

4 In which view should you sort a query?

5 Which field criterion is used to find records where no entry has been made in the specific field?

6 Complete the table by filling in the correct comparison operator for the described query.

Description	Operator
Used to specify more than one condition where the query results need to match only one of the conditions.	
Used to specify more than one condition where the query results must match all of the conditions.	
Used as a placeholder when specifying criteria.	

Independent practice activity

In this activity, you'll create and run a query. Then, you'll update data in the query and in its source table and add a field to that query. Next, you'll create a query that uses comparison operators and the AND condition. You'll change that query to use wildcards. Finally, you'll create a query that uses the Count function.

1 Open Orders.

2 In Design view, create a query, based on the tblOrderItem table, that displays Order ID, ProductID, and Quantity. Run the query.

3 In Datasheet view, modify the query result by changing the value of Quantity of product with Product ID 5 to 300.

4 Save the query as **qryPractice**.

5 Verify that the change is reflected in the tblOrderItem table.

6 Add a new field, curItemPrice, to the query qryPractice, and run the query.

7 Update and close the query.

8 Create a new query based on the tblProduct table that displays all the product names and unit prices for records having a Unit Price between $1.00 and $2.00. Run the query, and compare your results with Exhibit 5-6.

9 Delete the previous criteria, and display all the records where the Product Name begins with **Ce**. Close the query without saving it.

10 Create a new query based on the tblOrder table that displays the count of retailers having orders on the same date. (*Hint*: Use Count in the Total row for the field lngOrdRetailerID, and use Group By in the Total row for the field dtmOrddate.) Compare your results with Exhibit 5-7.

11 Close the query without saving.

12 Close the database.

Product Name	Unit Pric
Celery Seed (Whole)	$1.75
Celery Seed (Ground)	$1.50
Chives	$1.25
Annatto Seed	$1.23
Cinnamon (Ground) Extra High Oil	$1.99
Asafoetida Powder	$1.49
Anise Seeds	$1.49
Basil Leaf (Whole)	$1.89
Carob Powder (Raw)	$1.89
Basil Leaf (Ground)	$1.45

Exhibit 5-6: The query result after Step 8

CountOfIng(	Order Date
2	1/6/2006
1	1/8/2006
3	2/2/2006
1	2/9/2006
1	3/1/2006
2	3/6/2006
1	4/1/2006
1	5/6/2006
1	5/21/2006
1	6/11/2006
1	6/23/2006
1	7/7/2006
1	8/9/2006
1	8/11/2006
1	9/9/2006
1	9/22/2006
1	10/12/2006
1	11/1/2006

Exhibit 5-7: The query result after Step 10

Unit 6
Using forms

Complete this unit, and you'll know how to:

A Create forms.

B Create and modify forms in Design view.

C Sort and filter records by using forms.

Topic A: Creating forms

This topic covers the following Microsoft Certified Application Specialist exam objectives for Access 2007.

#	Objective
2.5.7	Create forms by using Layout view
2.5.8	Create simple forms

Database Forms

Explanation

A *form* is an Access database object that allows you to view, edit, and add data to a table. The datasheet view of a table shows you a grid of fields and rows. A form typically shows just one record at a time. The fields can be arranged on a form and labeled for clarity, as shown in Exhibit 6-1, and they can be made to look like familiar paper documents, such as invoices. The underlying table from which the field values come is referred to as the *source table*. Well-designed forms make a database program more effective and easier to use.

Form Views

There are three form views:

- Form View—The final form as it will be used. See Exhibit 6-1.
- Layout View—Looks like Form View, but you can move and format objects.
- Design View—The view for building the form, where you add fields and controls and define object properties. See Exhibit 6-2.

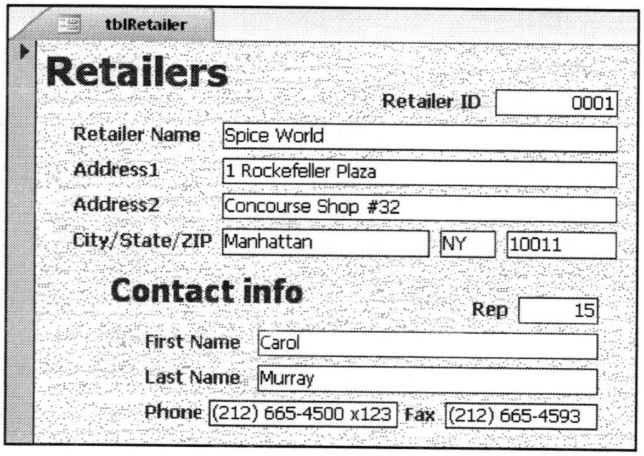

Exhibit 6-1: A sample Access form in Form View

Examining a form in Design view

You can create a form by clicking the Form button on the Ribbon, or by using the Form Wizard, or you can create a form from scratch in Design view.

To create a form or change its design, you can use Design view, shown in Exhibit 6-2. In Design view, a form contains three main sections:

- **Form Header**—Use this section to enter a heading that describes the form's purpose. This header appears at the top of the form for every record.
- **Detail**—The Detail section contains various controls, such as label and text box controls. Often, the detail section is all you really need.
- **Form Footer**—Use this section to enter information to display at the bottom of a form when it is previewed or printed.

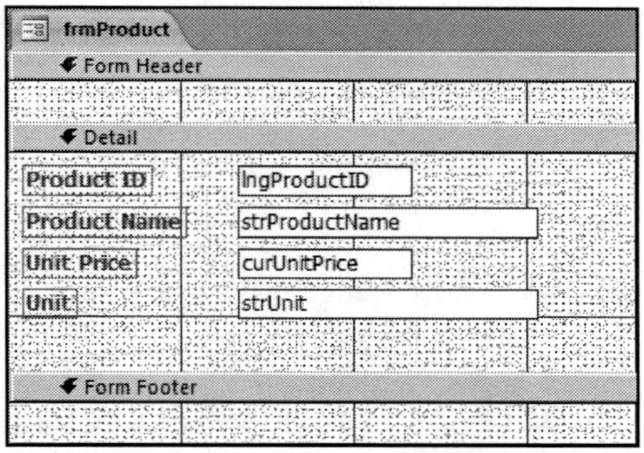

Exhibit 6-2: A basic form in Design View

When you open a form in Design view, two context-specific tabs appear: Design and Arrange, as shown in Exhibit 6-3 and Exhibit 6-4. These contain tools to add, modify, and arrange controls on the form.

The Form Header and Form Footer sections might not be visible when you open a form in Design view. To show or hide them, right-click the form and choose Form Header/Footer, or click the Form Header/Footer button on the Layout tab.

Form controls

Every object on an Access form is a control. A *control* displays data, allows you to edit data, or performs some action. Many controls, like text boxes, list boxes, and option buttons, can link to data in a source table. Other controls, like labels, shapes, and pictures, are used to make the form clear, organized, and attractive.

The following table describes some of the commonly used controls on the Design tab:

Control	Name	Description
	Label	Gives a description for the controls used in a form.
	Text box	Enters data such as numbers or text.
	Option button	Selects a single option from a set of options.
	Check box	Selects multiple options from a list of options.
	Combo box	Selects an option from a drop-down list.
	List box	Selects multiple options from a list.

Form Design view can also contain a Field List pane, which shows all the fields in the table on which the form is based. To display the fields, click the Add Existing Fields button on the Design tab.

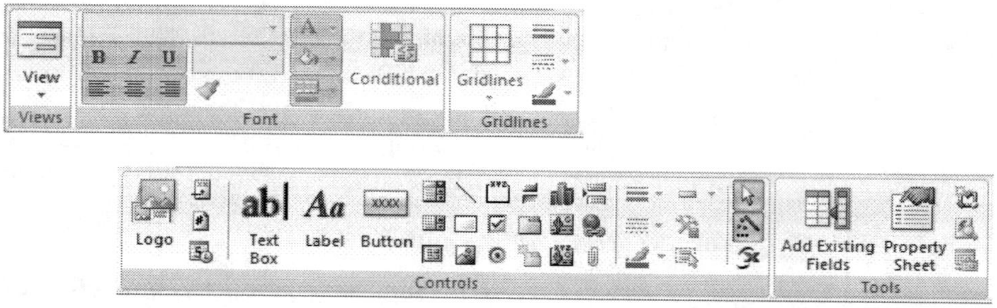

Exhibit 6-3: Form tools on the Design tab

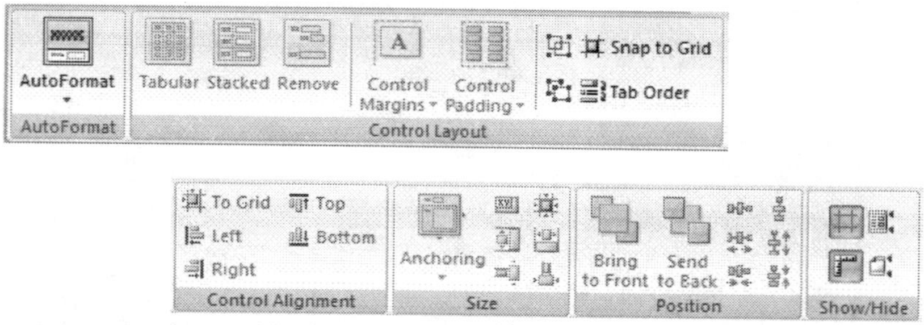

Exhibit 6-4: Form tools on the Layout tab

Do it!

A-1: Examining a form

Here's how	Here's why
1 Open CreateForm	From the current unit folder.
2 Open **frmProduct** in Design View	You'll examine a form.
3 Activate the Arrange tab	
4 Click 	(The Form Header/Footer button is in the Show/Hide group.) To show the Form Header and Form Footer sections.
Click Form Header/Footer again	To hide the header and footer.
5 Activate the Design tab	
6 Observe the Controls group	(As shown in Exhibit 6-3.) It contains controls and other form objects that can be used in forms.
7 Observe the form	The form contains the Detail section. The label controls—such as Product ID, Product Name, Unit Price, and Unit—are on the left side of the window.
8 Observe the text box controls	The field names appear in the text boxes. The form gets the values for these fields from the source table. You can see the values when you switch to Form view.
9 Click **Add Existing Fields**	 (In the Tools group.) The Field List pane appears on the right side of the window. It lists the fields that you can use on the form.
Click **Add Existing Fields** again	To close the Field List pane.
10 Close the form	Close without saving changes.

Basic forms

Explanation

If you're using the Form button to create a form, all fields in the selected table are included automatically in the form. Here's how to create a form by using this feature:

1 In the Navigation pane, select a table on which to base the form.
2 Activate the Create tab.
3 In the Forms group, click Form.

After you create the form, it displays in Layout view. The layout of a form created with the Form button is always columnar. A columnar form displays values in one or more columns, as shown in Exhibit 6-5. A tabular form displays values in a row and column format. After creating a form, you can arrange the controls to better suit your needs.

The form shown in Exhibit 6-5 contains label controls and text box controls. Label controls display the field names, and text box controls display the data in the fields.

Text box controls are an example of *bound controls*; they are linked to the fields of the underlying source table. Any change made in a bound control is reflected in the underlying data source. For example, if you're working in a form and you change data entered in a text box, the underlying field is also changed.

Label controls are an example of *unbound controls*; they are stand-alone controls that do not have a data source. Other unbound controls are lines, rectangles, and pictures.

Exhibit 6-5: A basic columnar form in Form view

Do it!

A-2: Creating a basic form

Here's how	Here's why
1 In the Navigation Pane, click **tblRetailer**	You'll select the underlying source table for a form.
2 Activate the Create tab	
3 In the Forms group, click the Form button	 A form opens in Layout view.
4 Save the form as **frmBasicForm**	Click the Save button and edit the name to read frmBasicForm. Click OK to save the form and close the Save As dialog box. The name appears in the Navigation Pane.
5 Click 	(The Form View button is on the window frame.) To switch to Form view.
Close the form	

The Form Wizard

Explanation

You can create a form by using the Form Wizard. In the Form Wizard, you can select the fields to display, the order in which they appear, a layout, and a style. The Form Wizard guides you through the steps necessary to create a form. Form Wizard helps you specify which fields you want in the form, whereas creating a basic form with the Form button automatically places all of a table's fields in the form.

To create a form by using the Form Wizard:

1. Activate the Create tab.
2. In the Forms group, click More Forms and select Form Wizard.
3. Select the table and fields that you want to display in the form. Click Next to move to the next step of the Form Wizard.
4. Select a form layout and click Next.
5. Select a style for the form and click Next.
6. Enter a title for the form and click Finish.

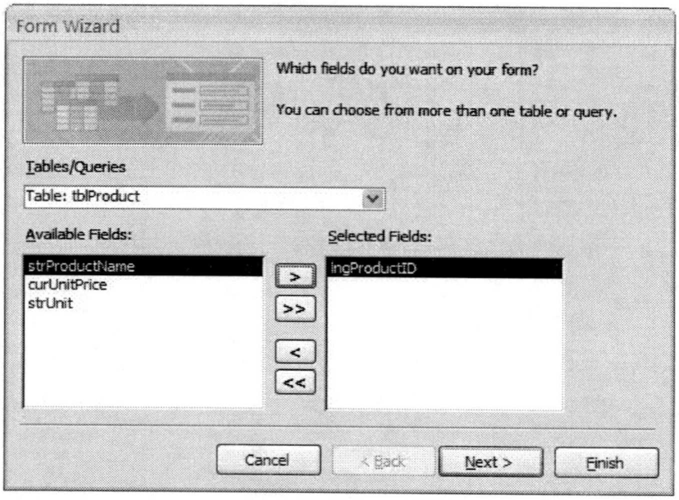

Exhibit 6-6: Selecting a table and fields in the Form Wizard

Do it!

A-3: Creating a form using the Form Wizard

Here's how	Here's why
1 Activate the Create tab	You'll create a form by using the Form Wizard.
In the Forms group, click **More Forms** and select **Form Wizard**	The Form Wizard opens.
2 From the Tables/Queries list, select **Table: tblProduct**	To specify the name of the table on which your form will be based. Under Available Fields, all fields of the tblProduct table are listed.
3 Under Available Fields, verify that **lngProductID** is selected	You'll add this field to the Selected Fields list.
Click [>]	(To add lngProductID to the Selected Fields list.) lngProductID appears in the Selected Fields list.
4 Click [>>]	To add all the fields to the Selected Fields list.
5 Click **Next**	The wizard now displays form layout options.
6 Verify that **Columnar** is selected	You'll create a form that uses columns.
Click **Next**	The wizard now displays various form styles.
7 From the style list, select **None**	If necessary.
Click **Next**	
8 Edit the What title do you want for your form box to read **frmFormWizard**	This will be the form's title.
Click **Finish**	The form appears in Form view, displaying the first record. The record is shown in a columnar layout.
9 Click [►]	To view the next record in the form.
Click [►|]	To view the last record in the form.
Close the form	The frmFormWizard is now in the Navigation Pane.

Topic B: Using Design view

This topic covers the following Microsoft Certified Application Specialist exam objectives for Access 2007.

#	Objective
2.5.1	**Create forms by using Design view**
2.7.1	**Add controls** • Add fields from tables as controls
2.7.4	**Format controls** • Change font color • Change foreground color
2.7.5	**Arrange controls** • Anchor controls
2.7.6	**Apply and change conditional formatting on controls**
2.7.7	**Apply AutoFormats to forms and reports**

Creating forms in Design view

Explanation

After creating a form, you can open it in Design view. You can add, remove, resize, and rearrange the controls. You can also create a new form from scratch in Design view.

To create a form in Design view:

1. Activate the Create tab.
2. In the Forms group, click Form Design.
3. In the Field List, click to show all tables.
4. In the Field List, expand the table you want to use, and then drag the fields you want to use to the form.
5. From the Controls group, drag the controls you want to use to the form.
6. Arrange the controls and set other layout options.
7. Save the form.

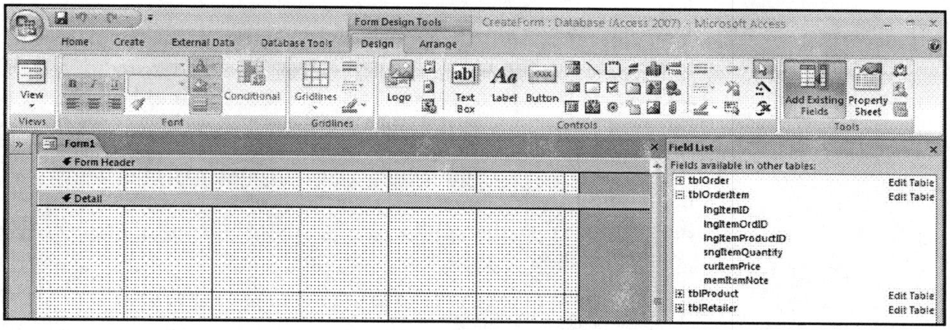

Exhibit 6-7: Detail from the Form View after Step 5 of the activity

Do it!

B-1: Creating a form in Design view

Here's how	Here's why
1 Collapse the Navigation Pane	(Click the double arrow in the upper right corner of the Navigation Pane.) So you have more room to work.
2 Activate the **Create** tab	You'll create a form in Design view.
In The Forms group, click **Form Design**	To open a new form in Design view.
3 Activate the **Arrange** tab	
In the Show/Hide group, click 	(Form Header/Footer.) To show the form headers and footers.
4 Activate the **Design** tab	
5 In the Tools group, click **Add Existing Fields**	To display the Field List.
In the Field List pane, click **Show all tables**	To display all of the tables available for inclusion in this form.
Click the plus sign to the left of tblOrderItem	To expand the field list for this table. Your screen should resemble Exhibit 6-7.

Working with controls

Explanation

You can move and resize controls in Design view. To place a new label control or a text box control in the form, you can select a field from the field list and drag it to the Detail section. The shape of the pointer changes to a field box. Both controls appear in the location to which you dragged the field.

When you select either control (label or text box), the shape of the pointer changes to a hand, and handles appear around the control. *Handles* are small, black rectangles around the control. You change the size of a control by dragging the handles, and you move a control by dragging the whole control when the pointer changes to a hand.

Anchoring controls

You can anchor controls on a form. If a user resizes a form, anchored controls remain in the same location and will resize if necessary. A control can be anchored to any of the four sides of a form, or it can be anchored to stretch across or down and across. To anchor a control:

1. Open the form in Design view or Layout view.
2. Select the control.
3. On the Arrange tab, in the Size group, click Anchoring.
4. Select the anchoring method.

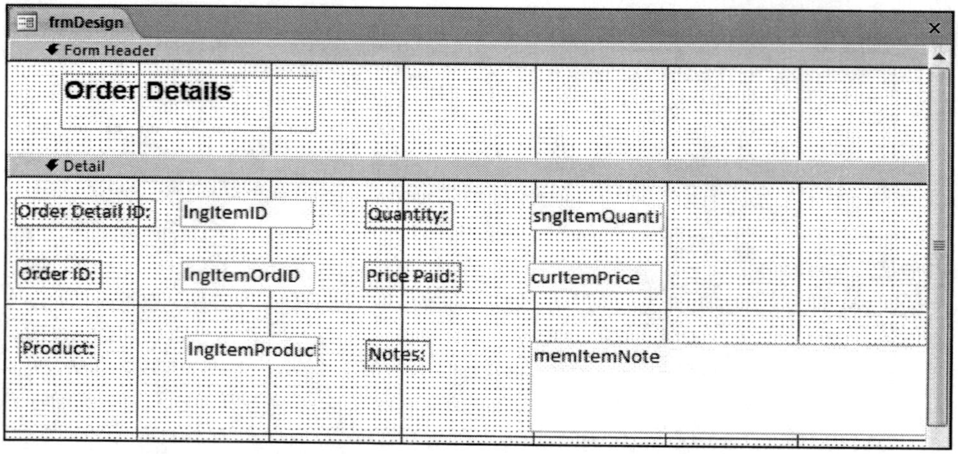

Exhibit 6-8: Controls added to a form

Do it!

B-2: Adding controls

Here's how	Here's why
1 Drag **lngItemID** from the Field List to the Detail section, as shown	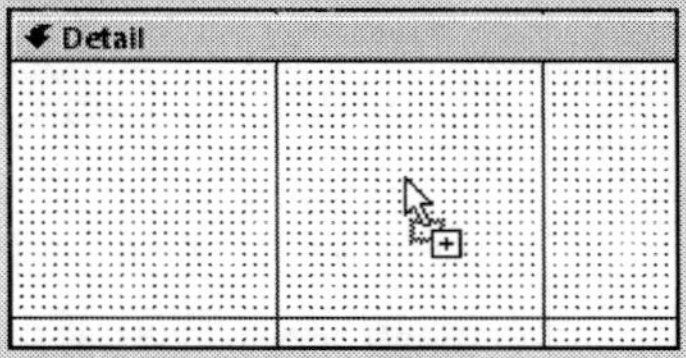 (The shape of the pointer changes.) You'll put a label control and a text box control on the form.
Observe the Detail section	A label control and a text box control appear.
2 Activate the **Arrange** tab	
Click **Anchoring**	In the Size group.
Select **Top Left**	To anchor this field to the top left corner of the form.
3 Insert the other fields from tblOrderItem, anchoring them to the Top Left of the form	As shown in Exhibit 6-8. Size and arrange controls as necessary. Use the tools on the Arrange tab to align controls.
Close the Field List	
4 Save the form as **frmOrders**	

Form control properties

Explanation

Each control in a form has a set of properties, which determine its appearance and behavior. All controls have a *Property Sheet*, which is used to change or customize the properties, such as Caption and Font Name. The Property Sheet contains five tabs: Format, Data, Event, Other, and All.

Section properties

Each section of the form also has its own properties and Property Sheet. For example, you can change the background color of the Form Header by changing the Back Color property on the Form Header section Property Sheet, shown in Exhibit 6-9.

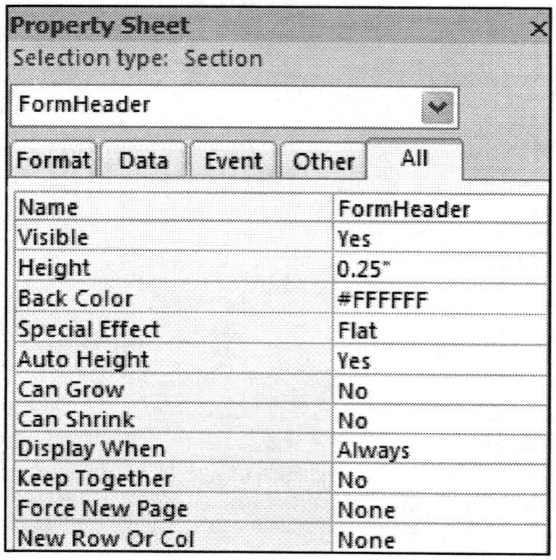

Exhibit 6-9: Fields on the Property Sheet for the Form Header section

Modifying section properties

To modify section properties:

1. Select the section of the form for which you want to modify the properties.
2. Activate the Design tab.
3. In the Tools group, click Property Sheet.
4. In the Property Sheet, change the section properties as needed.
5. Update the form.

AutoFormats

You can view a gallery of built-in formats by clicking the More button in the AutoFormats group on the Formatting tab. If you click a format, it is applied to the form and the gallery closes.

Do it!

B-3: Modifying properties

Here's how	Here's why
1 Click anywhere in the Form Header section	(Not on the label, though.) You'll modify the properties of the Form Header section.
2 Activate the Design tab	
In the Tools group, click **Property Sheet**	 (If necessary.) To display the Property Sheet.
3 Activate the Format tab	(On the Property Sheet.) The list in the Property Sheet displays Form Header. This list displays the name of the selected control or section whose properties are being modified. The Property Sheet displays the properties of the Form Header section.
4 Place the insertion point in the Back Color box	A button appears to the right of the Back Color box.
5 Click [...]	To display the Color palette and view the various colors.
Select any shade of yellow	To change the background color of the Form Header section to yellow.
Press ENTER	To make the change take effect.
6 Place the insertion point in the Special Effect box	A drop-down arrow appears.
Click the arrow	To display a list.
From the list, select **Raised**	You'll change the appearance of the Form Header section.
7 Close the Property Sheet	Click the Close button in the Property Sheet.
8 Click anywhere in the Detail section	You'll modify the properties of the Detail section.
9 Press F4	To open the Property Sheet.
10 Change the background color of the Detail section to orange	

11	Select the label **Quantity**	Notice the Property Sheet changes. You don't need to close the sheet between selections. The Format tab remains active.
	Edit the Caption box to read **Quantity sold:**	This will be the new caption of the label.
	Resize the label to accommodate the longer text	(If necessary.) Drag the right border of the box to the right.
12	Select **lngItemProductID**	
	Change the Fore Color to red	In the Property Sheet, place the insertion point in the Fore Color box. Then, click the button to display the list of colors, and select a shade of red. Then, press Enter.
13	Select **lngItemProductID**	(If necessary.) You'll see that font color and fore color are the same.
	In the Design tab, click the arrow beside Font Color	(In the Font group.) The color palette appears.
	Select **Automatic**	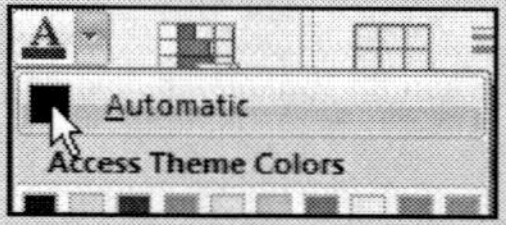 To change the color back to black.
14	Switch to Layout view	The modified form appears.
15	On the Format tab, click 	(In the AutoFormat group. The More button is at the bottom right of the group.) To display the Format gallery.
	Observe the formats	Each format applies one design to the Header section and a different design to the Detail section.
	Click anywhere on the form	To close the gallery.
16	Update the form	
	Close the Property Sheet	

Conditional formatting

Explanation

You can apply conditional formatting to text boxes and combo box controls on a form. A conditional format changes the appearance of a control if specific conditions are met. For example, you can create a conditional format that changes the font color in a numeric field if the value of that field falls below a level that you specify.

Conditional formatting can be applied on any of the following criteria:

- **Field value**—The format of a field changes based on the field's value.
- **Expression**—You can create a formula to change the format of a control.
- **Field Has Focus**—The format of a control changes when it is selected.

To apply conditional formatting:

1. Switch to Layout view and select the text field or combo box you want to format.
2. On the Format tab, click Conditional. The Conditional Formatting dialog box appears, as shown in Exhibit 6-10.
3. Under Condition 1, select the condition that must be met to apply the formatting: Field Value Is, Expression Is, or Field Has Focus.
4. Enter the values or the expression that define the condition, if necessary.
5. Select the format to apply when the condition is true.
6. If necessary, click Add to create another condition.
7. Click OK.

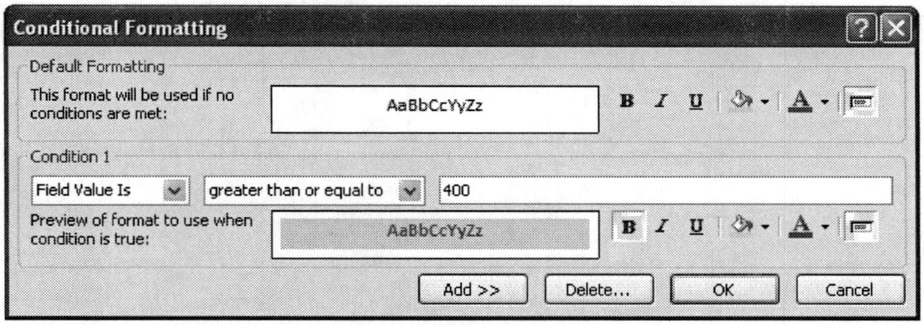

Exhibit 6-10: The Conditional Formatting dialog box

Do it!

B-4: Applying conditional formatting

Here's how	Here's why
1 Select the **Quantity sold** field	You'll apply a conditional format to this field.
2 On the Format tab, click **Conditional**	(In the Font group.) The Conditional Formatting dialog box appears.
Under Condition 1, verify that **Field Value Is** is selected in the first list	The condition will be based on the value in the field.
3 In the second box, select **greater than or equal to**	
4 In the third box, enter **400**	
5 Under Condition 1, click **B**	The Bold button. To make the text display in bold if the amount is greater than or equal to 400.
Make the Fill/Back Color yellow	Click the Fill/Back Color button and select any shade of yellow.
Make the font red	
6 Observe the preview window in the dialog box	It shows the appearance of the control if the condition is met: yellow background, and bold red text.
Click **OK**	To close the dialog box.
7 Navigate to the next record on the form	Click the Next Record button.
8 Observe **Quantity sold**	The value in the field is 400, so the conditional formatting takes effect.
9 Navigate to the next record	The value of the field drops, and the field resumes its default format.
10 Update and close the form	
11 Expand the Navigation Pane	Click the double arrow.

Topic C: Sorting and filtering records

This topic covers the following Microsoft Certified Application Specialist exam objectives for Access 2007.

#	Objective
5.1.4	**Sort data within forms**
5.2.4	**Filter data within forms**

Sorting records by using a form

Explanation

You can use a form to sort records in a table in either ascending or descending order.

If you want to arrange the records in ascending order, select the field on which you want to sort, and click the Ascending button in the Sort & Filter group. Otherwise, click the Descending button.

Do it!

C-1: Using a form to sort records

Here's how	Here's why
1 Open frmRetailer	The records are sorted based on the Retailer ID, which is the primary key.
Place the insertion point in the Retailer Name box	You'll sort the records based on Retailer Name.
2 Click 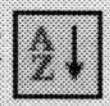	(The Ascending button is in the Sort & Filter group.) To sort the records in ascending order. You'll see the first record after sorting. The records are now sorted based on the Retailer Name field.
3 Navigate through records	The records are now sorted alphabetically by retailer name.
Return to the first record	

Filtering records by using a form

Explanation

You can selectively view the records in a form by using the Filter By Form feature. For example, you can set the filter to view the products sold in a specific location. The Filter By Form feature contains two tabs: Look for, and Or. The Look for tab is used to filter records. The Or tab is used to enter alternate values, which are displayed by using the Look for tab.

To apply a filter:

1. Open the form you want to filter on.
2. Activate the Home tab (if necessary).
3. In the Sort & Filter group, click Advanced and choose Filter By Form.
4. Enter or select the value for setting the filter from the available list.
5. Click Apply Filter.

Do it!

C-2: Using a form to filter records

Here's how	Here's why
1 Click [Advanced] and choose **Filter By Form**	(In the Sort & Filter group.) To display a blank frmRetailer form. A drop-down arrow appears next to the Retailer ID box. The Look for tab is activated at the bottom of the form.
2 Place the insertion point in the Retailer Name box	A drop-down arrow now appears next to the Retailer Name box.
3 Enter **S***	You'll view the records for those retailers whose names start with S.
Press TAB	In the Retailer Name box, Like "S*" appears. You're using the * wildcard operator to filter data.
4 Click [Toggle Filter]	To apply the filter. The first record in the filtered set of records appears. The bottom of the form shows the total number of filtered records.
Navigate through the records	All the retailer names start with S.
5 Update and close the form	
6 Close the database	

Unit summary: Using forms

Topic A In this topic, you examined a form in **Design view**. You also created a form by using the **Form** button. In this topic, you created a form by using the **Form Wizard**.

Topic B In this topic, you learned how to create a form in **Design view**. You created a customized form by moving, adding, or rearranging **controls** in the form in Design view. You also changed the appearance of a form by modifying its **properties**, including through the use of **conditional formatting**.

Topic C In this topic, you learned how to use forms to **sort** and **filter** records. You arranged records and worked with specific records by sorting and filtering records.

Review questions

1 Which view is used to create or modify a form?

2 What are the three main sections of a form?

3 Identify the following controls that can be used when designing forms.

Control	Name

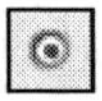	

4 What's the difference between clicking Form and using Form Wizard?

5 What is the difference between bound and unbound controls?

6 Which of the following is used to manage the appearance and behavior of a form control?

A Design tab

B Control handles

C Text box

D Property Sheet

7 How do you sort records by form?

8 How do you use a form to filter records?

Independent practice activity

In this activity, you'll create forms by using the Form button, the Form Wizard, and Design view. You'll create a title for a form, then sort and filter records by using the form.

1 Open Employee.

2 Create a columnar form based on the tblEmployee table by clicking the Form button.

3 Enter a new record in the form, as shown in Exhibit 6-11.

4 Save the form as **frmEmployeeDetails** and close it.

5 Using the Form Wizard, create a form based on the tblEmployee table.

6 Select all the fields in the table, and create a tabular form based on the Access 2007 style.

7 Save the form as **frmEmployee**. Compare the form to Exhibit 6-12.

8 Close frmEmployee.

9 Create a form in Design view using tblOrderItem.

10 Drag fields from the fields list to create the form as shown in Exhibit 6-13.

11 Sort the records in ascending order by Product. (*Hint*: You must be in Form view.)

12 Filter the records based on the Quantity field for values greater than 200. (*Hint*: Enter >200 in the Quantity field in Filter by Form.)

13 Save the form as **frmSalesSummary**.

14 Close the form and the database.

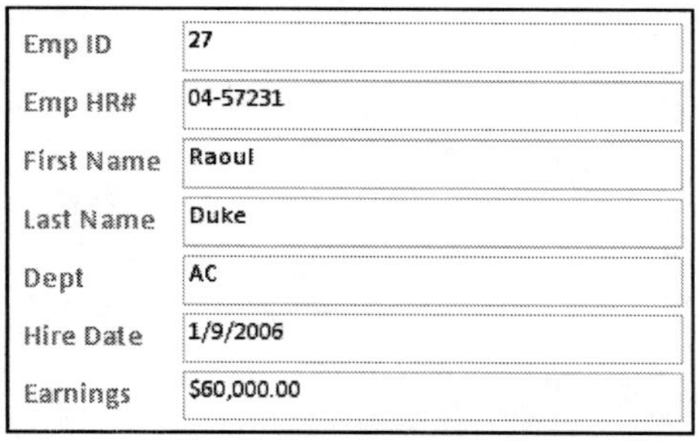

Exhibit 6-11: The frmEmployeeDetails form after Step 3

Exhibit 6-12: A sample of frmEmployee after Step 7

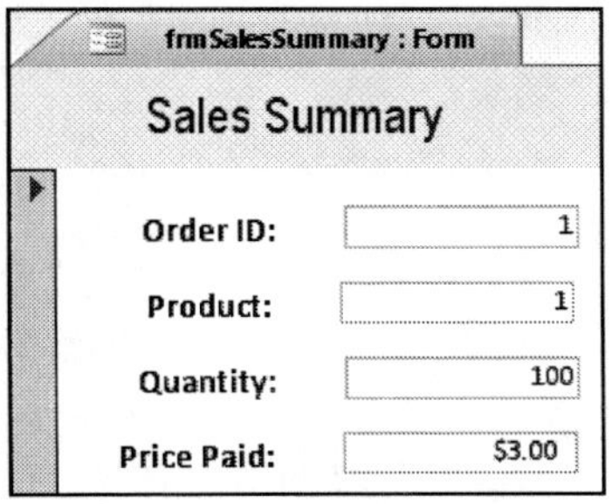

Exhibit 6-13: A sample of the Sales Analysis form after Step 11

Unit 7
Working with reports

Complete this unit, and you'll know how to:

A Create reports by using the Report button, Report Wizard, Design view, and Layout view.

B Group and sort records in a report, summarize information in a report, change the report layout and style, and print a report.

Topic A: Reports

This topic covers the following Microsoft Certified Application Specialist exam objectives for Access 2007.

#	Objective
2.6.1	Create reports as a simple report
2.6.2	Create reports by using the Report Wizard
2.6.3	Create reports by using Design view

Creating reports

Explanation

A *report* is an Access database object that presents data in an organized format suitable for viewing on screen or printing. Access creates a report by using the underlying source table or query, and Access can run calculations on fields and group data by specified criteria. In Exhibit 7-1, the Product Details report shows the records from the tblProduct table. A report is not used to enter or edit data.

The commonly used methods to create reports are using the Report button, using the Report Wizard, and using Design view. The Report button generates a report that contains all the fields of the source table. The Report Wizard prompts you to select the fields you want to include in the report. Design view gives you the flexibility to design customized reports from the ground up.

Viewing a report

There are four report views:

- Report View
- Print Preview
- Layout View
- Design View

To see an existing report, double-click the report name in the Navigation Pane. This opens the report in Print Preview. You can then switch to different views. You can also open a report by right-clicking the name and choosing Design view or Layout view. To see the Print Preview, you must have a printer driver installed on your computer. A report contains a report heading and various column headings for the fields.

You can view one page of a report at a time. In Print Preview, the pointer changes to a magnifying glass so that you can switch between Pages and Zoom views. In Pages view, one page of a report fits on screen, while Zoom view shows an enlarged report.

Outlander Spices

Product Details

Product ID	Product Name	Unit Price	Unit
1	Cassia	$3.00	2 oz
2	Catnip Leaf	$2.75	2.25 oz
3	Celery Seed (Whole)	$1.75	1 oz
4	Celery Seed (Ground)	$1.50	1 oz
5	Chamomile Flowers	$1.00	2 oz
6	Chili Pepper Powder	$2.00	2.25 oz

Exhibit 7-1: Product Details report in Print Preview

Do it!

A-1: Examining a report

	Here's how	Here's why
1	Open CreateReport	From the current unit folder.
2	Double-click **rptProduct**	To open the report in Print Preview.
3	Point to the report area	The pointer changes to a magnifying glass. You can use it to switch between Pages and Zoom views.
	Click in the report area	To zoom in on the report.
	Observe the Preview window	(As shown in Exhibit 7-1.) It contains both vertical and horizontal scrollbars that you can use to scroll through the report.
4	Observe the headings	The report heading is Outlander Spices Product Details, and the field headings include Product ID, Product Name, Unit Price, and Unit.
	Observe the end of the report	(Scroll down.) The current date appears on the left side.
	Point anywhere on the report, and click	To zoom out on the report.
5	Close the report	

Basic reports

Explanation

A basic report uses a columnar layout and includes all fields from one table. Here's how to create a basic report:

1. In the Navigation Pane, select the table or query on which to base the report.
2. Activate the Insert ribbon.
3. In the Reports group, click Report. A columnar report using all the fields opens in Layout view.
4. If necessary, use Layout and Design views, or Formatting, Layout, and Page Setup tabs to modify the report.
5. Save the new report.

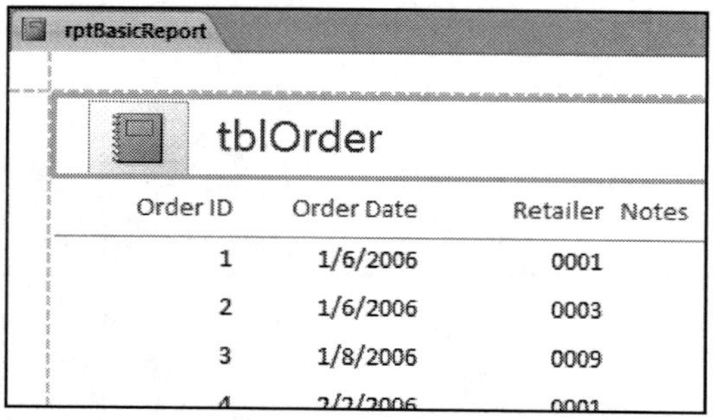

Exhibit 7-2: Part of basic report opened in Layout view

Do it!

A-2: Creating a basic report

Here's how	Here's why
1 In the Navigation Pane, select **tblOrder**	You'll base the report on this table.
2 Activate the Create tab	
In the Reports group, click Report	 To create the report and open a preview.
3 Save the report as **rptBasicReport**	It should look like Exhibit 7-2.
4 Click **OK**	To save the report. It appears in the Navigation Pane.
5 Close the report	

The Report Wizard

Explanation

When you create a report by using the Report Wizard, you can specify the fields you want to include in the report, and you can arrange the data by specifying a condition for sorting the records. You can also include summary calculations in your report. The Report Wizard guides you through every step of designing a report, from selecting fields to choosing a style for the printed page. The *style* defines the colors and fonts that will be used in the report.

To create a report by using the Report Wizard:

1. Activate the Create tab.
2. In the Reports group, click Report Wizard.
3. From the Tables/Queries list, select a table on which the report will be based.
4. From the Available Fields list, select the fields you want to include in the report. Click Next.
5. Select the options you need from the remaining steps of the Report Wizard.
6. Click Finish to exit the Wizard and create the report, or click Next to change grouping, sorting, layout, and style options before creating the report.

rptOrderDetails

lngItemOrdID	Product	Detail ID	Quantity	Price Paid	Notes
1					
	1	1	100	$3.00	
	11	13	50	$4.25	
	12	11	150	$5.50	
2					
	3	2	400	$1.75	
	7	12	20	$3.50	
3					
	5	3	200	$1.00	

Exhibit 7-3: Preview of the rptOrderDetails report

Do it!

A-3: Creating a report using the Report Wizard

Here's how	Here's why
1 Activate the Create tab	You'll create a report by using the Report Wizard.
In the Reports group, click **Report Wizard**	
2 From the Tables/Queries list, select **Table: tblOrderItem**	You'll create a report based on this table.
3 In the Available Fields list, verify that **lngItemID** is selected	
4 Click [>]	(The Add button is on the Report Wizard dialog box.) To add lngItemID to the Selected Fields list.
5 Click [>>]	(To add all the fields.) Now all the fields appear in the Selected Fields list.
6 Click **Next**	To move to the next step of the Report Wizard.
7 Select **lngItemOrdID**	You'll view records grouped on this field.
8 Click [>]	To add lngItemOrdID as a grouping level. In the thumbnail, lngItemOrdID appears in a separate box in the top pane. Notice that the Grouping Options button is now active.
9 Click **Next**	
Observe the Wizard	(The insertion point is in the first list.) You use this screen to specify the field on which you want to sort the records in the report.
10 From the first list, select **lngItemProductID**	To sort records by lngItemProductID in ascending order.
11 Click **Next**	To move to the next step of the Report Wizard. The various report layouts appear.
12 Under Layout, verify that **Stepped** is selected	To specify a layout for the report.
Under Orientation, verify that **Portrait** is selected	To specify the orientation of the report.
Verify that **Adjust the field width so all fields fit on a page** is checked	
13 Click **Next**	To move to the next step of the Report Wizard. The available report styles appear.

14 Select **None**	To specify a style for the report.
Click **Next**	
15 Edit the What title do you want for your report? box to read **rptOrderDetails**	To specify the report's title.
Verify that Preview the report is selected	To preview the report on screen before printing it.
Click **Finish**	You'll see a preview of the report, as shown in Exhibit 7-3. The title of the report is rptOrderDetails. The report shows records from the tblOrderItem table that are grouped by lngItemOrdID and sorted by lngItemProductID.
16 Close the report	

Creating reports in Design view

Explanation

Design view provides you with various tools to design reports. Tools include the Design tab, the field list, and the Property Sheet.

Design view

Design view is divided into the following sections: Report Header, Page Header, Group Header, Detail, Group Footer, Page Footer, and Report Footer. These sections control the location of the report elements. For example, the controls in the Report Header section appear at the beginning of a report. The following table describes each section:

Section	Description
Report Header	Appears at the top of the first page of the report. Use this section to show a company logo, the report name, or the date.
Page Header	Appears at the top of every page of the report. It appears below the report header on the first page. Use this section to show the field headings.
Group Header	Appears before every group of records. A group in a report contains records arranged together based on a specific field value. Use this section to display information, such as a group name, that applies to the entire group. For example, you can group records based on products sold to a customer, and the group heading can contain the name of that customer.
Detail	Appears once for every record. This section contains the main body of the report and is repeated for each record in the report's source table or query.
Group Footer	Appears at the end of a group of records. Use this section to show information, such as group totals, that is specific to each group.
Page Footer	Appears at the end of every page of the report. Use this section to show information such as page numbers and dates.
Report Footer	Appears at the end of the report before the page footer of the last page. Use this section to show information such as grand totals.

Do it!

A-4: Creating a report using Design view

Here's how	Here's why
1 Activate the Create tab	You'll create a report in Design view.
Click **Report Design**	(In the Reports group.) To open the Design view window. The three sections—Page Header, Detail, and Page Footer—appear.
2 Drag the Detail bar down as shown	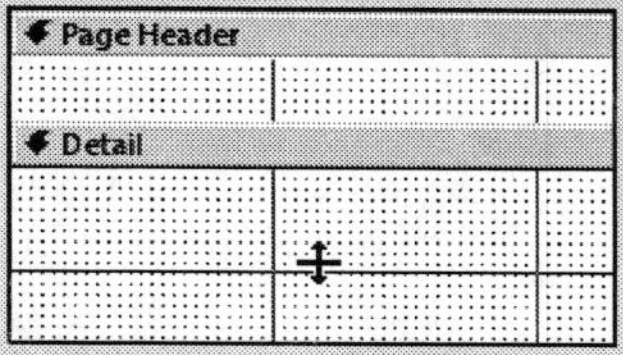 (To increase the size of the Page Header section.) The pointer changes to a double-headed arrow.
3 Activate the Design tab	If necessary.
In the Controls group, click *Aa*	To add a label control to the form.
4 Point in the Page Header area as shown	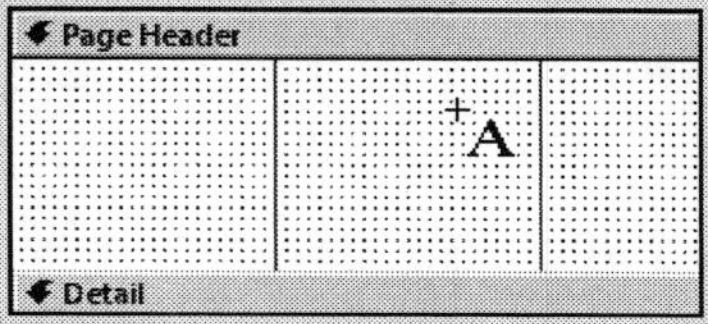
Drag as shown	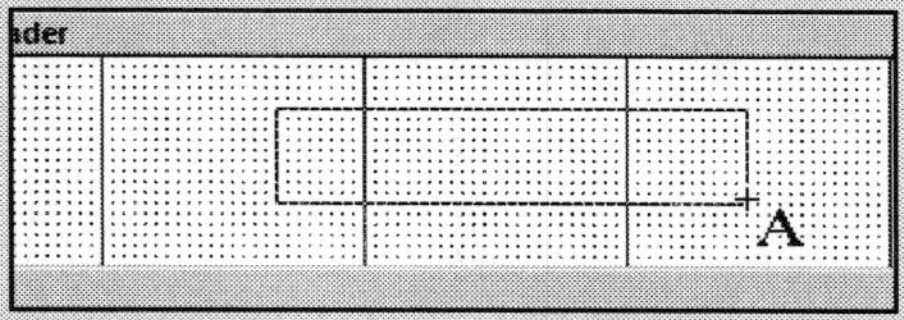
5 In the label control, enter **Retailer Details**	This will be the report's title.
Press ENTER	This will exit editing mode and select the control.
Make the title 14pt and Bold	Use the controls on the Design tab, in the Font group.
6 Show the Field List	(If necessary.) Click Add Existing Fields in the Tools group on the Design tab.
Expand **tblRetailer**	To see the fields in tblRetailer.

7 Drag **strRetailerName** from the field list to the Detail section, as shown	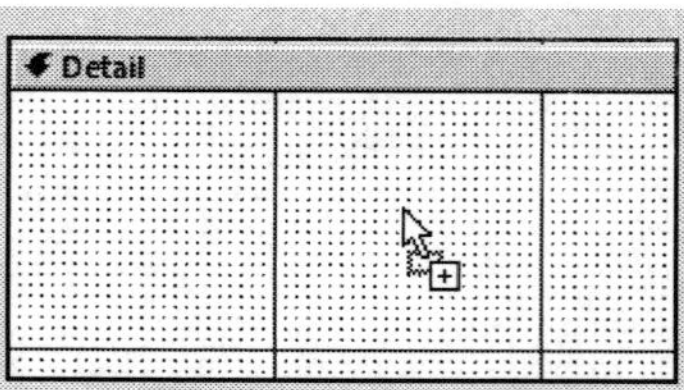
Observe the Detail section	A label control and a text box control appear.
8 Insert other fields as shown	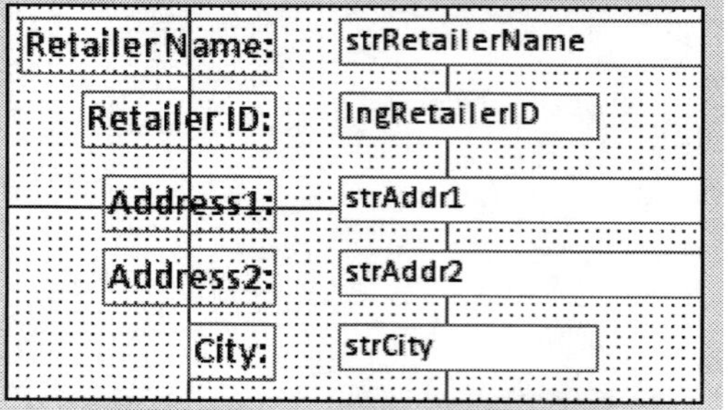 Use the alignment tools on the Arrange tab, and use the resizing handles to lengthen the name and address fields.
9 Save the report as **rptRetailerDetails**	
10 Close the window	Notice that rptRetailerDetails appears in the Navigation Pane.
11 In the Navigation Pane, double-click **rptRetailerDetails**	To view the report.
12 Close the report	

Topic B: Modifying and printing reports

This topic covers the following Microsoft Certified Application Specialist exam objectives for Access 2007.

#	Objective
2.6.5	**Create aggregate fields**
2.6.6	**Set the print layout** • Avoid excess pages, etc., basic print and layout skills • Design and arrange a report in Layout view
5.1.3	**Sort data within reports**
5.2.3	**Filter data within reports**

Modifying a report

Explanation

You can modify an existing report any time by using Design view or Layout view. Layout view has the advantage of showing immediately how the final report will look. You can do the following:

- Group records based on similar field values.
- Display the sum, average, minimum, and maximum values for each group or for every record.
- Sort or group the data by specific fields in a report.

Moving and resizing controls

You can change a report's appearance by changing the properties of the controls and sections in the report. You can also drag a control to a different place and resize it by using the resize handles.

Previewing the report

Print Preview and Report view are similar. Report view is mainly for use on the computer screen, while Print Preview is meant to give you an idea of how the printed report will look. You need to have a printer driver installed to use Print Preview.

Do it!

B-1: Modifying a report in Design view

Here's how	Here's why
1 In the Navigation Pane, double-click **rptOrderItem**	To open the report in Report view.
2 Click 	(The Print Preview button is on the window at the lower right.) To see what the printed report will look like. The title isn't centered, and it's not a very helpful title.
3 Switch to Design view	
4 In the Report Header section, edit the title qryOrderItem to read **Sales Details**	(Select the report heading, click inside the report heading box, and edit it.) To make the report's heading more meaningful.
Select the report heading as shown	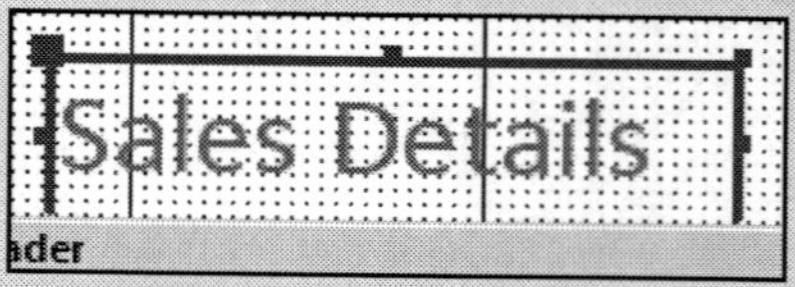 (Click anywhere outside the report heading, and then select the report heading box.) This is a label control. When you select it, handles appear around the text. Now you can change the size and location of the box.
5 Point to the border of the text box as shown	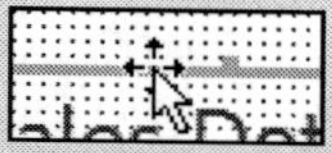 Point to the border but not to a handle.
Drag the title so it's centered over the fields	Leave the box selected.
6 Change the text color to white.	On the Design tab, in the Font group, click the drop-down arrow on the Font Color button and choose white from the standard colors. It will be hard to see at first.
Change the report header back color to a light shade of blue	Click anywhere in the header section to select it. On the Design tab, in the Font group, click the drop-down arrow on the Fill Color button and choose Light Blue or any other shade of blue.
7 Delete the logo	(To the left of the header.) It was put there automatically. Select it and press Delete.
8 In the Detail section, select all four fields	Hold down the Shift key while clicking each field.
In the Font group, click **Center**	To center the data under the headers.

9 Switch to Print Preview

10 Update and close the report

Layout view

Explanation

Layout view displays a report just as it would appear on paper. While in Layout view, you can move report items and configure the report for printing. You can see the effects of your changes immediately. To do this, switch to Layout view. Then drag and resize items on the report as desired.

Exhibit 7-4: Layout view

Do it!

B-2: Modifying a report in Layout view

<table>
<tr><th>Here's how</th><th>Here's why</th></tr>
<tr><td>1 Open rptProduct in Layout view</td><td>(Right-click the name in the Navigation Pane and choose Layout view.) You'll use Layout view to modify the design of an existing report.</td></tr>
<tr><td>Close the Property Sheet</td><td>(If necessary.) You won't use the Property Sheet in this activity.</td></tr>
<tr><td>2 Click the first number in the Product ID column</td><td>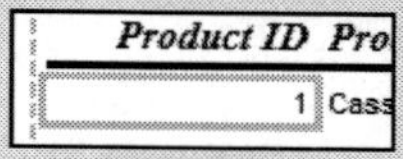

(If necessary.) An orange box highlights the field to indicate that it is selected.</td></tr>
<tr><td>Point to the left side of the field</td><td>The pointer changes to a double-sided arrow.</td></tr>
<tr><td>Drag to the right</td><td>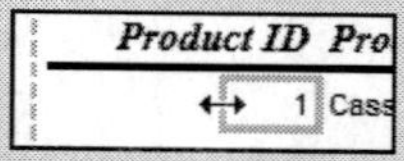

Reduce the field to approximately a third of its original size. The Product ID number uses a maximum of four digits, so the field does not have to be this large.</td></tr>
</table>

3	Drag the field to the right of the Unit field	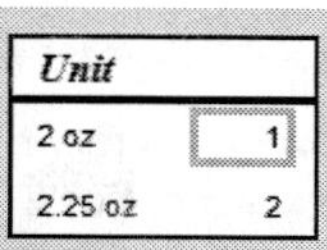 Point anywhere in the highlighted Product ID field, and drag to the right. The entire column moves to the right side of the report page.
	Move the column heading for the Product ID column	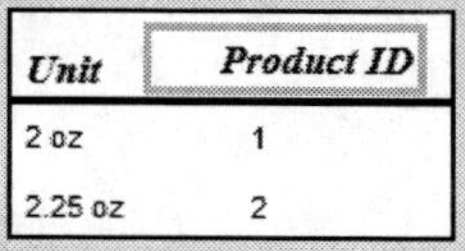 Click the column heading to select that field. Point anywhere in the field and drag to the right.
	Deselect the field	Click anywhere on the report page.
	Click the Product ID column heading	When you try to select the Product ID heading, the Unit heading is selected instead.
4	Activate the Arrange tab	You'll move the Unit column heading to the back.
	In the Position group, click **Send to Back**	To move the Unit column heading behind the Product ID column heading.
	Click the Product ID column heading	The field is selected now.
	Drag the field to adjust its position relative to the column	If necessary.
5	Update and close the report	

Grouping, sorting, and filtering records in a report

Explanation

You can group records based on a specific field to display all the records for that field at the same time. For example, you can group data by Order ID to display all records with the same Order ID together in a report, as shown in Exhibit 7-5. You can place a group name above each group, or place a field showing a total or other calculated value at the end of each group.

Sales Details

Order ID	Product	Quantity	Price Paid
2	7	20	$3.50
4	34	2	$17.00
5	23	25	$1.23
6	33	4	$14.89
11	30	20	$1.89
11	29	20	$12.49
14	25	45	$1.99
14	29	10	$12.49
16	4	10	$1.50
16	26	10	$1.49
16	2	25	$2.75
28	1	25	$3.00
28	12	25	$5.50
			$79.72

Sales Details

Order ID	Product	Quantity	Price Paid
28			
	1	25	$3.00
	12	25	$5.50
16			
	4	10	$1.50
	26	10	$1.49
	2	25	$2.75
14			
	25	45	$1.99
	29	10	$12.49
11			
	30	20	$1.89
	29	20	$12.49
6			
	33	4	$14.89

Exhibit 7-5: A report sorted and grouped on Order ID

Grouping and sorting records

To group and sort records, click the Group & Sort button on the Design tab. In the Group, Sort, and Total pane, specify the field and the sort order by which you want to group the records, as shown in Exhibit 7-6.

In the Group, Sort, and Total pane, you can click more to show options for group titles, headers, and footers. If you set any of these, a separate section for Group Header or Group Footer is introduced in report Design view, where you can place any information for a group of records.

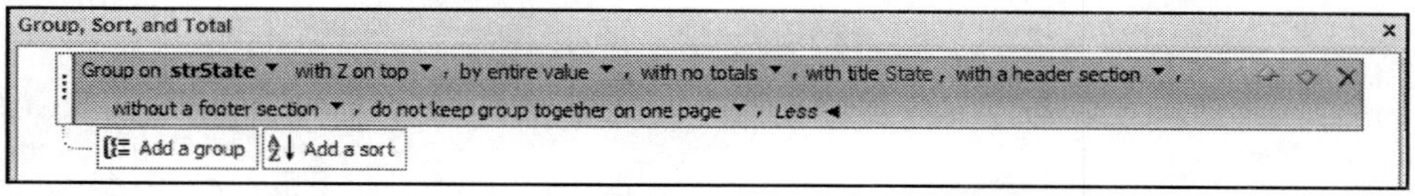

Exhibit 7-6: The Group, Sort, and Total pane with More options expanded

Filtering

To filter a report, switch to Report view or Layout view. Right-click a field and choose Text Filters or Number Filters, depending on the type of field. Then choose a filter type. Enter the filter criteria and click OK.

Do it!

B-3: Grouping, sorting, and filtering a report

Here's how	Here's why
1 Open rptOrderItem in Layout view	You'll use grouping to consolidate report details. Layout view will immediately display the effects of your actions.
2 Click Group & Sort	 (On the Report Layout Tools Formatting tab.) The Group, Sort, and Total pane opens at the bottom of the window.
Click **Add a group**	In the Group, Sort, and Total pane.
3 In the expression list, click **lngItemOrdID**, as shown	 You'll group records by lngItemOrdID.
4 Verify that the sort order is from smallest to largest	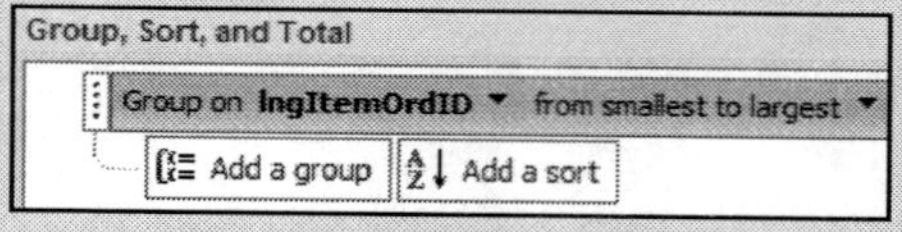
Observe the report pane	Records are sorted in ascending order based on their Order ID.
5 Click the arrow beside from smallest to largest, and choose **from largest to smallest**	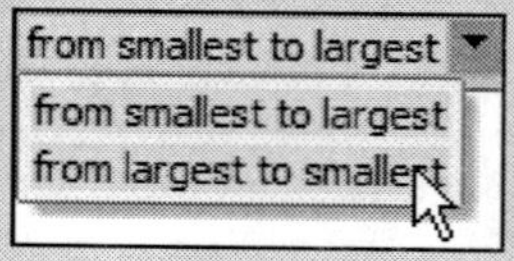 To reverse the sort order. The record list is reversed in the report pane.
Close the Group, Sort, and Total pane	

6	Right-click any value in the Quantity field	To display the shortcut menu.
	Choose **Number Filters**, **Greater Than…**	The Custom Filter dialog box appears.
	In the box, enter **25**	To filter for those records where the quantity ordered was 25 or greater.
	Click **OK**	To close the dialog box and apply the filter.
7	Observe the report	The report displays the details for orders where the quantity is greater than or equal to 25.
8	Right-click in the Quantity column	To display the shortcut menu.
	Choose **Clear filter from sngItemQuantity**	To remove the filter.
9	Update and close the report	

Adding summary information

Explanation

Calculated values for groups of records, such as totals and averages, are referred to as *summary operations*. You can add summarized data for a specific field by using either the Report Wizard or Design view.

To add a summary function in a report by using the Report Wizard:

1 On the Create tab, click Report Wizard.
2 Select the table or query on which to base the report, and add the desired fields. Click Next.
3 Add a field to the grouping level, and click Next.
4 Specify the sort order. Click Summary Options to open the Summary Options dialog box, as shown in Exhibit 7-7.
5 In the dialog box, check the summary value you want to calculate.
6 Click OK to close the dialog box and return to the Report Wizard.

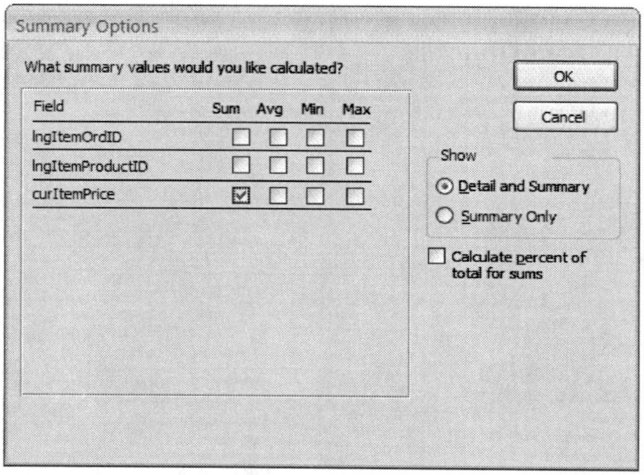

Exhibit 7-7: The Summary Options dialog box

Do it!

B-4: Adding summary fields using the Report Wizard

Here's how	Here's why
1 On the Create tab, click **Report Wizard**	(In the Reports group.)
2 From the Tables/Queries list, select **tblOrderItem**	You'll create a report based on this table.
3 Move the fields lngItemOrdID, lngItemProductID, sngItemQuantity, and curItemPrice to the Selected Fields list	(Select the fields and click the Add button.) To move the selected fields from the Available Fields list to the Selected Fields list. You'll view these fields of the tblOrderItem table in the report.
4 Click **Next**	
Select **lngItemOrdID**	(If necessary.) You'll group records based on this field.
Click [>]	
Click **Next**	In this step, you can specify the field by which you want to sort the records.
5 From the first list, select **lngItemProductID**	You'll sort records by lngItemProductID.
Click **Summary Options...**	To open the Summary Options dialog box, as shown in Exhibit 7-7.
Beside curItemPrice, check **Sum**	To calculate summary values for curItemPrice.
Under Show, verify that Detail and Summary is selected	
6 Click **OK**	To close the Summary Options dialog box and return to the Report Wizard.
7 Click **Next**	

Report layout and style

Explanation

The arrangement of data and labels in a report is referred to as its *layout.* When you create a report by using the Report Wizard, you can specify a layout and a style instead of using the Report Wizard's default layout and style.

To choose a report layout and style:

1. Select a layout for your report from the Report Wizard dialog box, as shown in Exhibit 7-8. The default page orientation is Portrait. Select the Landscape button to change the page orientation.
2. Click Next.
3. Select the desired style. Click Next.
4. Enter the title that you want to give your report.
5. Click Finish to preview the report.

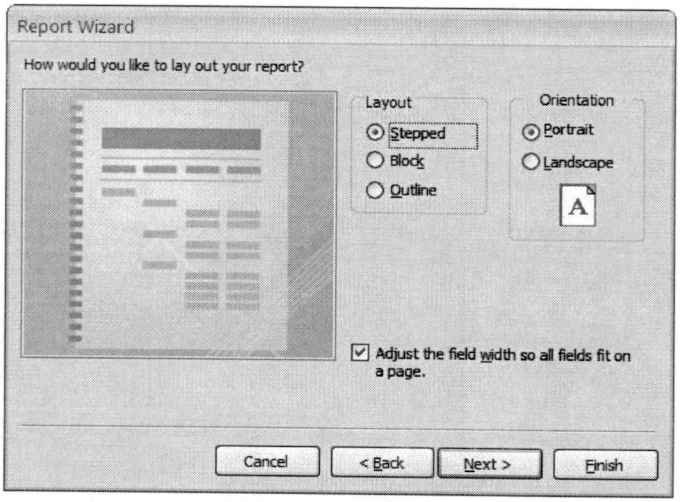

Exhibit 7-8: The Report Wizard with different layouts

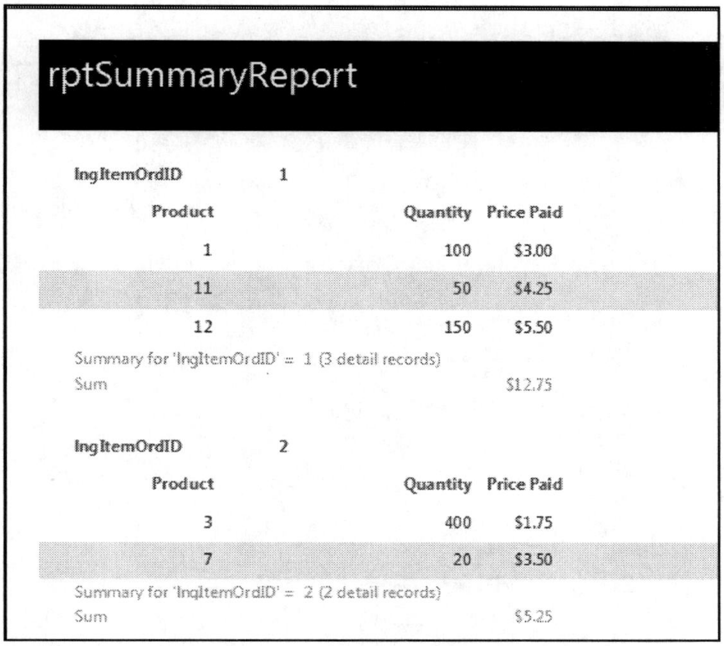

Exhibit 7-9: Layout and style applied to a report

Do it!

B-5: Modifying the layout and style of a report

Here's how	Here's why
1 Verify that the Report Wizard is open	
Observe the wizard	(Shown in Exhibit 7-8.) The current layout, Stepped, is the default layout.
2 Under Layout, select **Outline**	This will be the new report layout.
3 Under Orientation, verify that Portrait is selected	
4 Verify that Adjust the field width so all fields fit on a page is checked	
5 Click **Next**	
6 Select **Windows Vista**	To specify the style.
7 Click **Next**	
8 Edit the What title do you want for your report? box to read **rptSummaryReport**	This will also be the report's name. You can change the title later.
9 Verify that Preview the report is selected	
10 Click **Finish**	You'll see a preview of the report resembling Exhibit 7-9. The total quantity sold to each customer appears in the preview.
11 Close the report	

Printing reports

Explanation

When a report is displayed in Print Preview, the Print Preview tab displays two printing-related groups: Print and Page Layout. The latter should not be confused with Layout view. The Page Layout group offers some standard options for paper size, orientation, and margins.

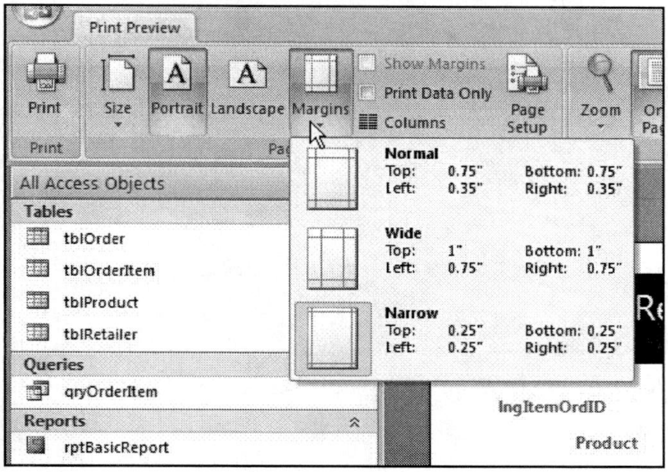

Exhibit 7-10: The Page Layout tab offers quick layout changes

If you need more precise control, the same options found in the Page Layout group can be found in the Page Setup dialog box (shown in Exhibit 7-11), but with text boxes for entering values. Open this window by clicking the Page Setup button or the Dialog Launcher in the Page Layout group.

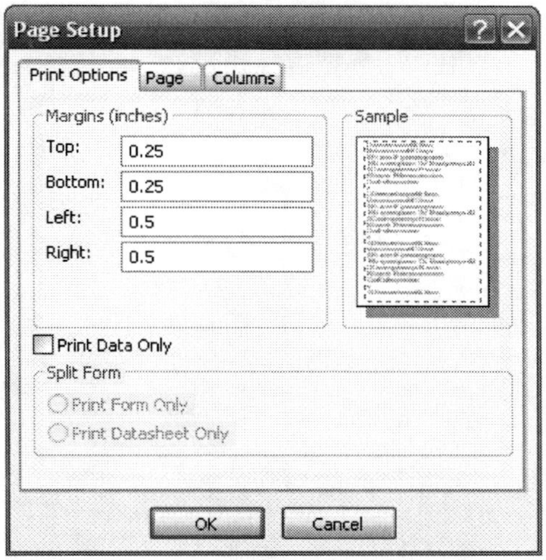

Exhibit 7-11: The Page Setup dialog box

If the page setup is correct, you can print the report by clicking the Office Button and choosing Print, or by clicking Print on the Print tab when the report is in Print Preview. To check printer options before printing, press Ctrl+P to open the Print window. Click OK in this window to send the job to the printer.

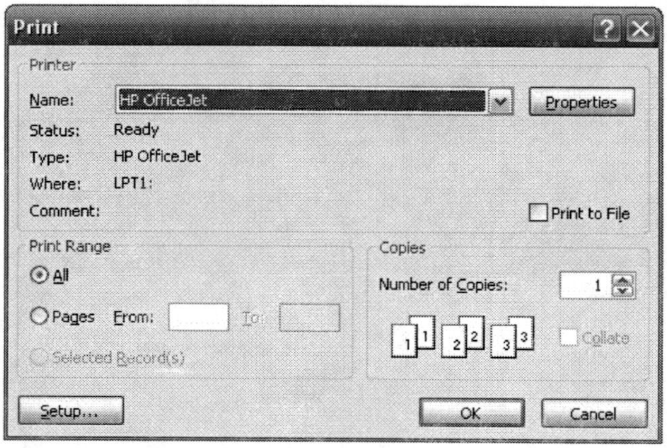

Exhibit 7-12: The Print dialog box

Do it!

B-6: Printing a report

Here's how	Here's why
1 Open rptSummaryReport in Print Preview mode	You'll review print options.
2 In the Page Layout group, click **Size** and observe the options	(On the Print Preview tab.) Standard paper sizes display.
Observe the options under **Margins**	Click the button.
3 In the Page Layout group, click 	(The Dialog Launcher is in the lower right corner of the ribbon group.) The Page Setup dialog box opens. It has three tabs: Print Options, Page, and Columns.
Observe the options available on each tab	
4 Close the Page Setup dialog box	
5 Click **Print**	 (On the Print Preview ribbon.) To open the Print dialog box, as shown in Exhibit 7-12.
6 Click **Cancel**	To close the Print dialog box.
7 Close the report	
Close the database	

Unit summary: Working with reports

Topic A

In this topic, you created a report by using the **Report button**. You learned that reports created this way automatically contain all the fields from the source table. You created reports by using the **Report Wizard**. You learned that the Report Wizard guides you through every step of designing a report. You also created a report by using Design view.

Topic B

In this topic, you **modified a report** in Design view and in Layout view. You also **grouped** records and performed summary operations on the records in a report by using the Report Wizard. You also learned how to select a style and a **layout** for a report. You also learned how to **print** a report.

Review questions

1 Name any of several ways to create a report.

2 How do you preview a report before printing it?

3 Which of the following is the default layout of a basic report?

A Columnar

B Tabular

C Portrait

D Landscape

4 When creating a basic report, where do you specify the table or query that contains the source data?

5 What is the procedure to group and sort records in a report?

6 If you want to add total amounts to a report, what feature should you use?

7 Which of the following is not a layout option for a report?

   A Stepped

   B Block

   C Justified

   D Centered

8 Name one way to print a report.

Independent practice activity

In this activity, you'll create a basic report based on a table and on a query. You'll use Report Wizard to create and configure a report.

1 Open CreateReportPractice.

2 Create a basic report based on the table tblOrderItem.

3 Save the report as **rptReportPractice** and close the report.

4 Using the Report Wizard, create a report based on the tblEmployee table. Use the following settings:

Item	Setting
Display the fields	lngEmpID, strEmpFirstName, strEmpLastName, strEmpDept, and curEarnings
Group the report by	strEmpDept
Sort in ascending order by	curEarnings
Summarize by calculating the average (Avg) of	curEarnings
Layout	Outline
Style	None
Specify title	Employee Details

5 After previewing the report, center the title and (if necessary) adjust field widths to show all data, then compare your report with Exhibit 7-13. (*Hint*: Adjust the report in Layout view.)

6 Preview the report.

7 Update and close the report.

8 Close the database.

9 Close Access.

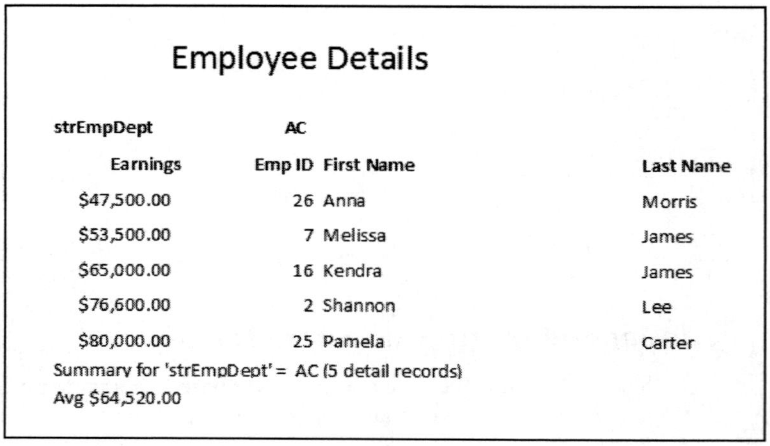

Employee Details

strEmpDept AC

Earnings	Emp ID	First Name	Last Name
$47,500.00	26	Anna	Morris
$53,500.00	7	Melissa	James
$65,000.00	16	Kendra	James
$76,600.00	2	Shannon	Lee
$80,000.00	25	Pamela	Carter

Summary for 'strEmpDept' = AC (5 detail records)

Avg $64,520.00

Exhibit 7-13: A sample of the Employee Details report after Step 7

Course summary

This summary contains information to help you bring the course to a successful conclusion. Using this information, you will be able to:

A Use the summary text to reinforce what you've learned in class.

B Determine other resources that might help you continue to learn.

Topic A: Course summary

Use the following summary text to reinforce what you've learned in class.

Unit summaries

Unit 1

In this unit, you learned that a **database** is used to store data in **tables**. You also learned about **fields** and **records**. Next, you learned how to **start Access**, and you examined the **Access window**. Then, you **opened a database** with **shared access** and examined the **Database window**. Finally, you learned how to use **Help options** to get information on Access topics.

Unit 2

In this unit, you learned how to create a database using the **Database Templates**. You learned about **Datasheet** and **Design** views for tables. Next, you created a table by using **Table Templates** and the **Table Wizard**. You also learned how to set the **primary key** and how to **add fields** in a table. Then, you learned how to **save** a table and **add records** to it. Next, you learned how to **copy**, **rename**, and **delete** a table. Finally, you learned how to create a **composite key**.

Unit 3

In this unit, you learned how to **modify a table** by **changing field names** and **deleting**, **inserting**, and **moving** fields. Then, you learned how to use the **attachment** data type. Then, you learned how to add a **totals row** to a table. Next, you learned how to use the **Find and Replace** dialog box. You also learned how to **undo** changes in a table. Finally, you learned how to **sort** and **filter** records in a table.

Unit 4

In this unit, you learned how to set the **Required**, **Allow Zero Length**, **Field Size**, and **Append Only** properties. Next, you learned how to set **input masks** for fields. Then, you learned how to set **Validation Text**, and **Validation Rule** properties for a field.

Unit 5

In this unit, you learned how to **plan** and **create** a **query**. You created queries by using the **Query Wizard** and **Design view**. You also learned how to **sort** and **filter** records in a query result. Next, you **modified** the **values** in a query result. Finally, you learned how to use **comparison operators**, **calculated fields**, and **aggregate functions** in a query.

Unit 6

In this unit, you learned how to examine a **form** in **Design view**. Next, you created a form by using the **Form Wizard**. Then, you learned how to create a form in **Design view**, **add controls**, and **modify** the **properties** of controls, including through the use of **conditional formatting**. Finally, you learned how to use forms to **sort** and **filter** records.

Unit 7

In this unit, you learned how to create a basic report by using the **Report** button. You also created reports by using the **Report Wizard**, **Design view**, and **Layout view**. You also learned how to **group records** and how to **add summary information** in reports. Finally, you learned how to select a **layout** for a report and print it.

Topic B: Continued learning after class

To get the most out of this class, you should begin applying your new skills and knowledge as soon as possible. Axzo Press also offers resources for continued learning. For more information, visit www.axzopress.com.

Glossary

Aggregate functions
Calculates values for a group of records by adding the values to the Total row of the query design grid.

AllowZeroLength property
Specifies that the field can contain null values.

AND comparison operator
Specifies more than one condition in the criteria and display the records that satisfy all of the conditions.

Append Only property
Specifies that a memo field can be added to by users, but that users cannot delete or change existing field data.

Bound controls
Controls that are linked to the fields of the underlying source table. Any change made in a bound control is reflected in the underlying data source. Text box controls are an example of bound controls.

Comparison operators
Adds criteria to a query to view records based on multiple conditions.

Control
An object in a form that displays data, allows users to edit data, or performs some action.

Data value
An item of data.

Database
A collection of data or information. An example of a simple database is a phone book that contains the names, phone numbers, and addresses of individuals and businesses.

Database management program
An application that stores and organizes data and makes data retrieval efficient.

Datasheet view
Displays data in a tabular format, containing rows and columns. Datasheet view helps users scroll through records and add, edit, or view data in a table.

DefaultValue property
Assigns a default value for the field, even if nothing is entered in the field.

Design view
Gives users complete control over the table's structure. Used to change the design of a table by adding or changing field details.

Entity
Any object that has a distinct set of properties.

Expression
A combination of symbols—identifiers, operators, and values—that produces a result. An expression can include the normal arithmetic operators for addition (+), subtraction (-), multiplication (*), and division (/).

Field
A specific type of information that applies to all items listed in a table.

FieldSize property
Specifies the maximum number of characters that can be entered in the field.

File format
The specific format in which each application stores data. By default, Access 2003 creates databases in the Access 2000 file format.

Filter
A set of conditions applied to data to view a section of data.

Filtering
The process of temporarily isolating a subset of records that satisfy certain criteria you specify.

Form
An Access database object that allows users to view, edit, and add data to a table. The datasheet view of a table shows a grid of fields and rows, while a form typically shows just one record at a time.

Form Wizard
Creates a form that prompts users to select the fields to be included, the order in which the fields will appear, a layout, and a style for the form.

Format property
Specifies the display format for data in a field.

Group
Organizes database objects through shortcuts.

Handles
Small, black rectangles around a control. Used to change the size and position of a control.

Index
Arranges data in the ascending order of value in a field and to find data in tables. An index in Access is similar to the index of a book, which is used to locate information.

Input mask
Defines how data should be entered in a field, and also determines the type of data and the number of characters.

Input Mask Wizard
Creates an input mask based on the built-in input masks in Access.

Layout
The arrangement of data and labels in a report.

Macro
Automates frequently performed database tasks, such as printing a set of weekly reports.

Menu
Contains commands to perform a set of related tasks.

Module
Automates and customizes database operations. Modules are programs written in Visual Basic.

Multiple-field index
Based on two or more fields in a table, such as First Name and Last Name fields.

Null value
A value that indicates missing or unknown data in a field.

Objects bar
Located in the left pane of the Database window, it shows various database elements, or objects, such as tables, forms, and queries.

OLE Object data type
Links to objects created in other applications, such as Microsoft Word.

OR comparison operator
Specifies two conditions in the criteria and displays the records that satisfy either of these conditions.

Pivot Chart view
Displays data graphically in Datasheet view.

Pivot Table view
Aids in analyzing data.

Primary key
A field that uniquely identifies each record in a table.

Property inheritance propagation
Feature that enables users to update the properties of an existing object when the properties in the underlying table have been changed.

Property sheet
Changes or customizes properties of a form, table, query, or report, such as Caption and Font Name. The property sheet contains five tabs: Format, Data, Event, Other, and All.

Query
A database object that retrieves data based on criteria from one or more tables and displays it.

Record
A single set of related data values.

Record selector
The small box to the left of each record in a table that navigates through the records. The record selector points to the currently active record and indicates its status. The icon for the record selector changes based on the status of the record.

Relational database
Any database that uses an RDBMS to organize data. This database can have multiple tables that contain data about various entities, such as products, sales, or customers.

Relational database
A type of database in which data is organized in the form of related tables. In related tables, one or more fields are linked to fields in another table. This link ensures that users can enter only those values that have corresponding entries in the other table.

Report
An Access database object that presents data in an organized format suitable for viewing on screen or printing.

Report Wizard
A feature that creates a report that prompts users to select the fields they want to include.

Required property
Specifies a field that cannot contain null values. If the Required property is set to Yes, a value must be entered in the field.

Row selector
Indicates the active row with a black triangle in Design view.

Single-field index
Based on one field in a table. This index helps users find and sort data in tables that contain large amounts of data.

SmartTags property
Specifies actions—such as sending e-mail, scheduling a meeting, or showing a calendar—for the data values in the fields.

Sorting
The process of organizing records in a meaningful way so that users can retrieve data in the order they wish.

Source table
The underlying table containing the data that provides the field values in a form.

Spelling checker
A tool that uses a built-in dictionary to check the spelling of words.

Status bar
Located at the bottom of the window, it displays the current status of ongoing tasks.

Summary operations
Calculated values for groups of records, such as totals and averages. Users can add summarized data for a specific field by using either the Report Wizard or Design view.

Table
A database object that consists of a collection of records that store data.

Task pane
Located at the right side of the window, it contains shortcuts to frequently performed tasks.

Template
A pre-defined database structure provided by Access.

Title bar
Contains buttons users can use to change the window size or close the window.

Unbound controls
Stand-alone controls that do not have a data source. Use unbound controls to display information (such as labels), lines, rectangles, and pictures.

Validation rules
Check data that has been entered into a field and verify that it matches the conditions for the type of data, the data format, or the number of characters that can be entered in a field.

Validation Text property
Displays a customized error message when the validation rule is not satisfied.

Wildcard operators
Placeholders that specify criteria in query conditions to retrieve multiple values There are two frequently used wildcard operators: the question mark (?) and the asterisk (*). The question mark is used to substitute for a single character. The asterisk is used to substitute for any number of characters.

Index